SAMAN... BIRCH

So far Samantha Birch is the author of one book. This one.
She's written about dresses, bridesmaids and cake toppers for
Brides and *You & Your Wedding*, and regularly contributes to
the likes of *GLAMOUR* and *Love Baking* – often while eating
cake in her pyjamas. She lives with her husband in a chaot-
ically untidy flat in Letchworth, which she pretends is an
artfully unkempt writer's loft in St. Albans.

For more information on Samantha, her writing, books and
events, follow her on Twitter @SamBirchWriter. For the best
in handy wedding tips and advice, get over to @
HighStreetBride. You can also join her on Facebook.com/
The-High-Street-Brides-Guide/503367949687522 or visit
her website sam:-birch.co.uk.

The High-Street Bride's Guide

SAMANTHA BIRCH

A division of HarperCollins*Publishers*
www.harpercollins.co.uk

Harper*Impulse* an imprint of
HarperCollins*Publishers* Ltd
77–85 Fulham Palace Road
Hammersmith, London W6 8JB

www.harpercollins.co.uk

A Paperback Original 2014

First published in Great Britain in ebook format by HarperImpulse 2014

A catalogue record for this book is
available from the British Library

ISBN: 9780007592487

Set in Minion by FMG using Atomik ePublisher from Easypress

To Darren, for our life together

CHAPTER 1

The Basics

The best ways I know to save big

I love giving people good news. That's probably why this is my favourite bit. Because this is where I tell you that an amazing wedding – yes, designer dress included – isn't just for actresses and heiresses.

You *can* say your vows in a catwalk gown so beautiful it reduces your mum to tears (and not because she paid for it). You *can* style a reception so stunning your guests won't believe you didn't hire an A-list planner. And you *can* sprinkle the day with personal touches that make everyone feel like you gave them special attention before they even got there. *Without* spending a house deposit on it. Honest.

All you need is to be a little more savvy, a little more organised and a little more open-minded than your average pop princess. And that's not too much to ask for a beautiful day you'll show pictures of to your granddaughters, right?

The Golden Rules
There are four top secrets to saving money on your wedding – and I'm not suggesting you go for all of them. Some of them won't be

for you, and some of them don't go together, but if you can even manage one or two, in all honesty, these are the biggest, simplest ways to save the maximum amount of money before you even start planning.

1. 'Tis the Season

Summer weddings are the most expensive. Fact. Everybody wants one because you've got more chance of sunshine – but you'll pay hundreds of pounds more to get hitched in the warmer months, and since we live in good old Blighty, chances are the heavens could open on you anyway.

So consider the overlooked options: pretty spring with its freshly sprung flowers and vintage-y golden lighting; autumn with its colourful rush of auburns, oranges, yellows, reds and golds; or winter – my personal favourite for the excuse to cover everything in glass and glitter, bright reds and sparkling silvers, and wrap up in cuddly faux fur. Because who cares if, baby, it's cold outside and the rain is pouring down when you're posing under a super-cute brolly or huddled round a crackling fire with a toasty mug of rum and hot chocolate?

2. Monday's Child is Full of Grace

I'll give you one guess which day of the week is most popular for weddings. Ding ding ding, we have a winner! Saturdays, what a shocker. No-one needs to take any time off work, everyone can sleep off their aching heads on Sunday, and all your little cousins and second cousins can be there because they don't need to skip Maths, English and Double Geography.

So you can imagine the amount you'll save by being prepared enough to let everyone know months in advance – I'd suggest 12 months, to be exact – that they'll need to book some time out instead.

The midweek big day is a cunning budget-stretcher and politics-sidestepper in more ways than one. Think about it: all Mum and Dad's random friends from work won't be able to get the time off, for starters. That's a few scoops off the catering bill, plates and cups off the hire price, favours off the list and chairs that don't need covering – carry on at this rate and you'll be able to book a smaller venue…

3. Three Hundred's a Crowd

You can do this. I believe in you. Don't let fear hold you back and other supportive clichés. Because cutting the guest list is a task so stressful that many a smart, savvy bride has buckled under the pressure, but just look back at tip number two if you've ever even thought it's not worth keeping your numbers under control. And that's just the start of the savings: there are the invites and orders of service, wine during the photos and wedding breakfast, champers for the toasts and then some. But here comes the good news again: there *are* ways of keeping your total as svelte as a runway poser without putting everybody's noses out of joint.

Elope. Seriously. If both of your friends and family won't kill you, hotfoot it off to Gretna Green and get the job done right now. No? Okay, so you wouldn't need this book if running away together was really on the cards, but now we're agreed that there are going to be more than three or four of you, that means there will come a time when you have to look closely at who's fattening your list up. Guess what? It's now. ·

If it's work people who are ballooning your invitees, opt for the friends and family wedding. Tell them you're envisioning an intimate day with parents, siblings and friends you've had since you were nine, and then go and make it happen. If more and more friends and family push their way onto the list as the wedding develops, there's no need to keep it a secret – just make sure your colleagues feel like the good guys for not adding to your stress levels.

Have you been to three weddings a year for the last decade, and now ended up with 60 happily married people on your list who you never see? Don't make yours a 'payback' wedding – and the same goes for friends you haven't heard from in ages. Take a deep breath, and be realistic: there are no hard and fast rules, but don't be afraid to admit to yourself which friends and couples have drifted out of your life and probably won't be in touch after your nuptials.

Think about it: if you really want to reconnect with people who have been out of your life for years, is a day when you're going to be flitting from table to table for thirty seconds at a time really the best way? Or would you be better off calling them up for a visit a couple of months after the honeymoon, when the dust has settled?

4. Give it a Whirlwind

Don't even think about this one if you're not good under pressure. *Do* consider it if you're looking for a way out of the giant wedding you and your other half never wanted. Presenting the whirlwind wedding: getting married in six months or less – often in under three months. Depending on your venue, you may find that offering to plan your day in next to no time saves you hundreds of pounds.

The pluses: you'll be married (hooray!) and you'll have to be decisive. If you panic when given too many options and have a tendency to drag decisions out, this is one way to make sure you both say 'yes' more often than 'maybe…'. You'll also find a lot of venues that offer whirlwind packages are happy to hook you up with an in-house planner at no extra charge – and they can help you with the likes of recommended local suppliers. Your package may even include things like basic stationery, chair covers and a master of ceremonies too, so there should at least be a little less on your plate.

The minuses: you've got to have a seriously open mind to pull this off. Unless you're going for an intimate wedding, there's a good chance not all your guests will be able to make it at short notice. Also, the band or DJ you've had your heart set on might turn out to have been booked up months in advance – *and*, *gulp*, most wedding dress shops prefer six months minimum to order, fit and adjust your dress. So your choices on a few things could be limited – but as you'll see in the coming chapters, there's more than one way to find everything you're looking for.

Negotiating for Dummies

Come on, get out from behind the sofa – soft furnishings won't protect you from the fact that there's some bartering to be done. If you want to save maximum money without sacrificing style, that is – and let's be honest, that's why you're here isn't it? But trust me, this isn't a quick-fire 'going, going, gone' scenario, and no-one's going to bump up your bid if you scratch your nose – you can take your time, mull every offer over and apply as much or as little pressure as you're comfy with. And not only do you not have to look your opponent in the eye, you don't even have to *meet* them.

We only paid full price for about four things for our whole big day, and I didn't even have to pick up the phone to make the other prices plummet. For me, email is king. You may have noticed that I'm at home with a keyboard – definitely more so than a high-pressure sales call – so I used my way with the printed word to my advantage. Pick your weapon of choice – email, phone or face-to-face – and work in the way that suits you. But bear in mind these handy hints as you do:

Do Your Research

Know the industry-standard prices for the area you're into – read super-handy guidebooks (ahem, 'hem) and Google local hair-dressers/beauticians/cake makers etc. to get rough prices, high and low, so you know when you're being swindled. Okay, so the stuff at the lower end of the scale might not be up to scratch – maybe the icing on those cupcakes is a little lobsided or everyone comes out of that hairdresser looking like the Cookie Monster, whether they want to or not, but that's irrelevant, because you're *not* going to let the corner-cutting types near your wedding. You're just going to use the fact that they exist to make it *cheaper*.

Know Your Supplier's Status

Now you know your numbers, contact a handful of your preferred suppliers. These are the guys you really *would* want at your W-day. Explain your big-day using details that will make a difference to them: it's off-peak, it's on a weekday, it's a last-minute thing, you only need them for a couple of hours and not the usual full day, you have a million people coming (and this could be their chance to bake a million cookies...) – all of these affect them. If their books are looking empty for the next two months and you're offering them a job, they're likely to take it at less than their usual rate. If you want them on a Wednesday when they'd normally be twiddling their thumbs, they're more likely to jump at the chance for some extra moolah, even if it's not as much as they'd get on a Saturday. Explain that you're not flush and you're getting quotes from a few places – competition can only be a good thing – then ask them for their best price.

Photographers are a specialist area: they get their names out there via wedding magazines and blogs, and both of those want original, quirky weddings with a lot of personal details, so – and this won't be the last time I say this – Describe. Your. Day. That'll get your very-visual snapper on-side with the whole idea of shooting your totally awesome theme, not to mention getting the press potential popping up in front of their peepers. And the more they want the job, the more they'll be willing to bargain with you.

Keep an Open Mind

The truth: you might not get your #1 dream supplier at your can-it-really-be-real price. But you *are* likely to get someone similar for a number that's not too much of a stretch. How? In one of three ways:

1. A few of the suppliers you contacted come back with good discounts. Dive right in to your favourite, take them at the price they've quoted and you're away.

2. Only one or two of them can offer you any kind of discount, and it's not as much as you'd hoped for. This is where those nightmare low-priced, wonky, blue-haired suppliers come in. Quote one of the low-par prices, saying this is what you can get your preferred supplier's service for, and see if they can match it or at least get any closer to it. Hooray – higher-quality supplies/service for lower-quality rates!

3. If no-one can offer you a reasonable discount, one option is to decide whether to ditch said supply altogether – how much do you really want chair covers? – while the other route is to ask for recommendations. Most good businesspeople know the competition, and will have done their own price research. They'll be able to put you in touch with competitors who offer a similar or slightly lesser service (like someone talented without the experience to prove it) at a less expensive price than theirs. And *that* gives you a lower price point from which to get the whole negotiating process going again with the new name.

It's seriously that simple. Admittedly it might be tougher if you've found somebody seriously niche – no-one was budging on the price of the three-foot-high light-up '*love*' sign we wanted, since you don't exactly see those every day – but as long as there's competition for what you're after (there are always plenty of bakers, hairdressers, make-up artists and photographers), there's going to be room for monetary manoeuvre. Just try it.

CHAPTER 2

The Venue

Eat, drink and be merry for less

I'm starting here because this is likely to be your biggest outlay. Between hiring the place, getting your registrar over and feeding and watering everybody, it's one part of your day that can quickly pile on the pounds.

Before You Start
If you haven't read my golden rules back in The Basics, now's the time do it – trust me, not-so big spender, they're absolutely worth it. Once you've decided whether to go off-season, get hitched on a weekday, keep your guest list trim or get married in three months flat, then we'll talk.

You Little Fibber
It's a sad fact that the word 'wedding' sounds like 'kerching!' in the minds of some venues and suppliers – they know you're planning the perfect day, and they think you'll sell your car to pay for it. An industry tip that gets bandied around is to tell them you're

planning a 'family party' – and it can work, too, if you've got the nerve to stick to it.

When I first started planning my big day, I chickened out and owned up – worried that they'd try and stick me with a big bill when I turned up in a white dress – but the experience was an eye-opener that might make you think twice about being quite so forthcoming.

Here's how my little tale of woe went: I found a beautiful venue online and emailed them asking what it would cost to hire a room, have a barbecue for about 100 people and bring in a DJ for dancing later. I said it was a 'family party' since the plan was to have my ceremony and all the actual matrimonial stuff at the registry office, then rock up there later.

Back came the chirpy reply from an enthusiastic salesperson, attaching reams of barbecue menus and quoting me a fee our budget liked. Ecstatic, we called her up, agreed to come and see the place and what do you know? There we were in the entrance hall a few days later. And that's where it happened: she asked me what kind of 'family party' I was having, and I cracked: 'Well it's a wedding reception, but it's just the party, not the ceremony or anything.'

Before I could blink she'd told me that they couldn't do barbecues for weddings, only three-course meals, and that we couldn't have the room we wanted – funnily enough the only ones we *could* now have were more expensive.

Why? I didn't have to have a room that was certified for weddings – we'd already have had the ceremony before we got there. And I wasn't changing the plan for the party one iota – we didn't want posh chops on the BBQ or some kind of lovey-dovey wedding DJ. That didn't seem to matter though – she *was* changing it, in no uncertain terms, and it was going to cost us – wait for it – *double*.

So it's up to you if you've got the guts to try your luck – and if you do, make sure you read your contract carefully. Also keep in mind that this won't fly if you're planning to accost the registrar and turn up in your room of choice – it has to be certified if you want it for your ceremony.

But if you can get away with it, you could end up having your reception somewhere you never really thought you could afford, and just the way you like it – not to mention that if they're anything like our lot was, you could be getting it for half their normal nuptial rate.

Flexi Time
If you're stuck on a traditional wedding venue – the country house, the big hotel – you're going to have to be smart or it's going to cost you. And even then, there will still be some sky-high hire prices or required bedroom rentals that will take certain venues out of the running. Wherever you get married, though, there are, as always, a few general rules that could help you keep the costs down.

The Ceremony
Let me say right from the start that you'll almost always pay more to have your ceremony at your reception venue. You'll generally pay over the odds to have a registrar come out to you to start with, and then you've got to tack on a cost of room hire that usually blows the registry office's out of the water. Sundays and Bank Holidays are the most expensive wherever you walk down the aisle, but even midweek nuptials can be as much as twice the registry office price if you want your registrar off-site.

Do the numbers, but unless your reception venue is out in the sticks, even if you have to hop in your dad's car or pre-book a taxi to get you from 'I do' to 'woohoo!' it's likely to work out cheaper than doing it all in one place – and believe me, no-one will notice what car you arrive in now the Prosecco's out and rings are on fingers.

The Reception
If you manage to find a place that comes in within budget and you've got the time to suss them out, don't sign anything until you can

tell whether they're flexible. There are all sorts of ways to save on your reception as long as you can get your go-between to go for it.

Culinary Expertise

The three-course, sit-down meal is the most expensive way to feed your five thousand, hands down. Yes, it suits a formal gathering, and silver service always feels special, but weigh up how much you need it when it can be two or three times more than some other options.

If you *have* to have it, though, be clever: ask if you can serve your canapés as starters with the pre-reception drinks, or, if you really want to stay on your venue's good side, they tend to prefer it if you opt for the wedding cake instead of dessert.

One option that's similarly genteel, super-popular and certainly worth asking your venue about is **the classic afternoon tea.** Bottles of pop and pots of *chai* are immediately cheaper than wine, wine, wine – but a Prohibition-era theme could see to that if you still want to serve some bubbly. Then there are the snacks themselves – a few finger sandwiches, satisfyingly stodgy scones with clotted cream and pretty cakes won't set you back nearly as much as tomato soup followed by the customary dried chicken and chocolate mousse that everyone pushes around to save room for cake.

In summer, a **barbecue** is a fun option, and only requires minimal staffing on the venue's part. The winter equivalent is the **hog roast** – not so easy on the eyes maybe, but there'll be no complaints from your guests' satisfied stomachs. And before you ask, yes, you can get vegetarian options – just ask your venue what they can do.

Buffets are the usual antidote to all the pomp and circumstance of the post-speech feed-with-servants, and just like the BBQ and hog roast, having people queue for their food doesn't mean you can't have all the fun of a seating plan – if anything, it gives those single ushers and maids something to chat about before they find their tables.

Not all buffets were made equal, though – there are a few different ways that you can do this. First up: a very British classic. This is your **traditional buffet** – all triangle sarnies, cocktail sausages and little pieces of cheese and pineapple on sticks. Beef it up with the likes of pizza slices and Indian or Chinese snack selections – and add some jelly and ice-cream if it's not too hot for a touch of retro fun.

Second, if your venue is the kind where you supply your own caterers, talk to them about something a bit different, or pull it together yourself. **Sweetie tables** have been big for a while now and aren't showing any signs of going anywhere. They're literally pretty tables spread with Cath Kidston-esque linen, glass jars filled with sweets and maybe a few cakes – we used our wedding cake as the centrepiece. Seriously, think how easy it would be to nab some containers (save, hire or buy from your local **Asda** or **Wilkinson**), then raid your local pick 'n' mix (we miss you, Woolworths!) or snap up grab-bags of your fave sweets and go fill 'em up.

On a similar theme – but requiring more input from your caterers, who will *love* your ingenuity – 'build-your-own' bars are popping up all over the place. Featuring everything from top-your-own jacket potatoes or ice creams to fill-your-own fajitas, brainstorm fave foods with your groom and go from there. Anyone for stack-your-own sandwich with baguettes, cobs and rolls, or build-a-burger with different meats, veggie bean patties, relish and sauces?

Finally, if you've got chefs among your rellies who are vying for a part in proceedings, make the most of their talents instead of padding out your ceremony with a million readings. You can specify your favourite eats or just allocate some cooks sweets and some savouries, then have each one **bring a labelled dish** – preferably one that can be served cold unless your venue doesn't mind you using their ovens – along with serving utensils so everyone can dig in on the day. Now *that's* what I call a family feast.

Bottle It

Drinkies are a sizeable cost that you two don't have to carry alone – it's not uncommon for couples to put in for a drink or two per guest before the wedding breakfast, a drink or two during and a glass of bubbly for the toasts, then open up the bar for the rest of the night and let everybody pay for their own.

Keep costs down by talking corkage with your venue and bringing your own bottles, or opting for less expensive beverages like house wine, and clinking glasses with Prosecco or Buck's Fizz over straight champers. You could even wheel out your own big-day punch or cocktail – just make it with more juices than alcohol and stick to the affordable stuff.

Little Extras

We'll get into this in the Style Details chapter, but for now I'll just say that you need to keep an eye out for what's included with your wedding package. Some venues will throw in tidbits like pretty chair covers – great if you can get them, but the question is, do you really *want* them? Unless their seating really ruins your theme or is all-out supremely hideous, at around £3 to £5 per chair on average, that's another £300 to £500 for 100 people. Before you put your John (or Joanne) Hancock on anything, talk about ditching the bonus bits and trimming down the bottom line.

The same goes for stationery. It's common for an all-in package to include bits like menus and place names. Ask to see samples, and find out how much of your quote they'll be setting you back. If they do the job and they're easy on your margins, go with them by all means, but scout out local printers beforehand to check you couldn't get them cheaper – and more personalised – yourself.

Then there's VAT. It's not uncommon for venues to quote an off-their-head price that sounds spectacular until you realise they're not counting the tax. Be clear on whether it's included or you could end up with a bumper bill that's due the week before your big day.

Beyond the Norm

If you're open to suggestions for your reception venue, or you're looking for somewhere quirky and *so* you, there are ways to nigh-on cancel all your hire costs. Remember: as long as you do the legal bit in a certified room or registry office, you can do the rest wherever you want.

At one particularly lovely wedding I went to, the bride and groom had the ceremony the week before, then on the day the bride's dad acted as registrar. He read some of his own words while the bride and groom exchanged rings and said how they really felt in front of close friends and family. In case you're wondering: not a dry eye in the house.

Whether you have the ceremony on the day or a more intimate get-together just before then, doing the 'I do's separately to dancing the night away blows your venue options wide open.

The Grand Theme of Things

So we've established that you can hold your reception wherever you want once the papers are signed – and that means a **friend's house or back garden** if you happen to know someone with plenty of space, and even more patience. Remember though, if you throw your bash at a mate's place or go with the marquee option you'll usually have more choice of suppliers, but you have to be prepared to handpick them yourself – and to sort out the cleaning afterwards.

If you'd rather stick someone else with the washing up, don't forget you can break out your first dance at any party venue. If you're having trouble finding anything realistic when you Google 'wedding venues' in your area, swap in 'party venues' and see what happens.

You'd be surprised how many weird and wonderful places regularly set aside rooms for celebrations: aquaria; boats; cinemas – especially indie ones; courts (yes, you read that right); galleries; libraries; museums; sports clubs; theatres; tourist attractions; unis and colleges outside term time; zoos...

But there are even more options beyond those. Sometimes options neither you nor even the owner has ever thought of. At the end of the day, where you hold your do is about where you can negotiate hire of, even if they don't normally do it.

How about a **loft or apartment** that's available for short-term rental? There are all sorts of sites that offer up people's homes in popular cities such as London or Edinburgh – just check with the homeowner whether it's okay to bring a fair few friends back.

Then there are **photo studios** – they're often up for hire for freelance photographers and can be great if you're after a real blank canvas. Because they're often owned by arty types, you can find some amazing buildings with exposed brick or beams for a cool, contemporary backdrop.

Wherever you find yourself, even if they don't usually hire out to anyone at all, if you like the space and can see it transformed for your big day, what's the harm in asking? You've got the best chance of getting a green light from the manager if you stick to these three simple rules:

1. The Time is Right
When is the place you're pitching your wedding to likely to have quiet periods, and how can you capitalise on that? If you're after a summer or weekend wedding, for example, try university or college buildings – they don't have the student spend while they're all back home working summer jobs, but you can bring in a few extra bucks.

If you're happy to go with a weekday wedding, how about a wine bar on a quiet Monday night? Just remember, you'll have to suss out a good time to get all your decs set up and your entertainment in – many places will let you get them sorted the night before, but check to avoid delays on the day.

2. What's in it for Them?
If your off-piste venue serves food and drink, agree a minimum spend *instead* of a hire price. You're bringing them 100 people

who are planning on drinking from mid-afternoon into the night – you shouldn't have to pay another £1,000 for the privilege. If they're not that kind of outfit, it's time to talk about hire prices. Shocking fact: these are likely to be lower in slow periods and higher in busy ones – well I never.

Alternatively, if they're a smaller business, think about whether there's a skill you can offer them – filmmakers, photographers or writers could do recordings, shots or copy for their PR purposes. Bloggers or tweeters with a decent following could promote or review them. It doesn't even have to be you – maybe a willing family member could offer their services as your wedding present.

Whatever you agree on though, make sure you're covered. I've said it before and I'll say it again: ensure VAT is included in the price you're quoted, and make sure you get yourself a contract in writing.

3. It's Not the Size, It's What You Do With It

This is just one reason why the size of your guest list counts: it alters your venue-spotting strategy. The best way to pin down an unusual place? Look for venues with that all-important separate hire space.

Let's take restaurants as an example. If you've got a super-size group of, say, more than 100, you can try your luck with asking to hire out the whole place, but in some cases you'll find they want you to cover the cost of all the custom they'd have got in and out of the door over the periods you want them for. That can mean – and I'd sit down here if I were you – as much as £10,000 or more if you want to hire them over lunch *and* dinner. For guest lists of that size, you're better off looking at a bigger building to start off with – somewhere like a university that's built for large numbers of people, and will have a big enough room just idly going spare.

Let's call a medium group between 40 and 100. For this sort of size you've got the chance to downsize to the type of medium-to-small place that has a spare floor. Leaving downstairs free for other customers to come and go as they please means you won't have to cover the costs of what they'd usually eat or drink, and places that haven't been hired out for weddings before will be keener to help you if they don't have to turn away regulars.

If you can keep your numbers intimate – in some cases as small as 10 or 15, or up to 50 to 70 if you're lucky – you can simply hire a room. Plenty of eateries offer secluded dining areas for private parties where you can celebrate completely undisturbed, and since they rarely charge, an agreement RE food and drink spend should pretty much do the trick.

The only issue with this smallest option is entertainment – check with your venue about whether they'd be happy to clear out tables and chairs for dancing and mingling when you're done eating, or whether they have the facilities for you to pipe in some of your own playlists. If not, can you bring your iPod and hook it up to a set of speakers? Or maybe you've got an unexpected way to while away the time in mind – stand-up comedy, close-up magic or a silhouette artist and some good old-fashioned conversation, anyone? Check out the Entertainment section for more ideas.

Crucial Money-Saving Questions
Take this check-list along to your venue and make sure you save maximum monies.

If we were to hold our wedding here in the next three months/ on a weekday/off-peak, say, in winter, what discount could you offer us on the standard rate?

Is it possible for us to bring in our own food or caterers?

If not, what dining options do you offer besides the three-course wedding breakfast? Is it possible to substitute that for a buffet/ barbecue/hog roast/afternoon tea?

If not, could we serve the canapés in place of our starter, or our wedding cake in place of dessert?

Would you be averse to us setting up our own additional sweetie/ potato/sandwich bar before the wedding breakfast/as the wedding breakfast/later in the evening?

Is it possible for us to bring in our own drinks, and if so, what do you charge for corkage?

If not, what would our costs per head look like if we served house wine instead of the more expensive selections, and Prosecco/ Buck's Fizz instead of champagne?

What is included with our package? Is it possible to remove the stationery/chair covers/other smaller details and reduce the price?

Do you have the facilities for us to use an iPod or other MP3 player for music later in the evening, or would we need to bring in a band/DJ?

Do you have a list of preferred suppliers who might be willing to offer us a preferential rate if we book with you?

Is VAT included with all the costs you've quoted?

CHAPTER 3

The Dress

Designer, high-street or affordable W-day brand – you can afford a gorgeous gown

If you've ever stood in front of a full-length bridal shop mirror, all clipped and pulled in all the right places, with your mum, sister and best friends nodding encouragingly as you gaze at the perfect fit of your dream dress, then unless you're reading this section for a bit of fun I'm guessing you know the heartbreak of being handed that tiny bit of paper with more noughts on than a Stateside catwalk.

But hold back the tears, ladies. You *can* feel that beautiful again. In a dress that's actually in your price range this time. It might be a dress with a designer label in the back of it, or one you've just been handed by the seamstress who stitched it to your exact measurements. It might arrive at your door hand-delivered and wrapped in tissue paper, or you might find it the traditional way – jumping up and down in your friendly neighbourhood bridal boutique.

There are plenty of ways to look amazing on your big day without selling your engagement ring to pay for it – all you have to do is keep an open mind, and pick the method that suits you best.

Before You Start

There are a few pointers that apply to almost every place you look for a dress, and they're worth considering if you want to maximise the luxe without paying out the megabucks.

First, the length. It's a general trend you'll notice that shorter gowns tend to be cheaper. Whether it's just because they use less fabric or because longer wedding dresses are more popular by tradition, if you can get away with a shorter dress – maybe at a low-key registry office wedding, on a summer day, or if a Fifties theme is your cup of tea – you'll often end up with a totally gorgeous gown for a much more purse-friendly price.

Second, the simplicity. Keeping your dream dress simple opens up more options for how to get hold of it, as you'll see in the rest of the chapter. But you'll also find that a clean-cut satin dress that's not all ruffles, lace and embellishment is often less expensive than something more full-on, even straight off the hanger – and you can understand it: more materials and more labour are needed to get a glitzier gown spot-on, and that's reflected in the cost.

Third, the colour. White, cream or ivory are of course the most popular swatches for your average I-doer. And yes, there is a difference between the three, as you'll be told over and over during your dress-shopping escapades. But blush shades have been creeping onto bridal catwalks for years – often light pinks, peaches and lilacs. Wedding maven Vera Wang has even sent dresses in deep reds, browns and black down her catwalk. Going for a shade less travelled is a fantastic way to open up all kinds of doors to a tinier bridalwear budget, as you'll see below. The question is: do you dare?

The Traditional Route

If you're finding there's nothing within your budget in any of the bridal shops, trust me: it's them, not you. There are a lot of boutiques that stock dresses within a particular price range

– £1,500 to £2,500 isn't uncommon – but there *are* great designers who pride themselves on creating beautiful bridal gowns at affordable prices.

The trick is to do three things: ask your boutique on the phone what their price range is before you even book the appointment; ask them to *only* show you dresses within your budget on the day; and know your designers, so you can spot the names that don't mean uninviting your groom's whole side of the family.

Prices will vary by individual dress, so it's still worth asking your boutique to limit what you try on to your preferred numbers, but in general, the below labels create a whole lot of chic styles for around £500 or less.

Alfred Angelo

Most of Alfred Angelo's gowns are classic or princess. They're even behind the Disney Fairy Tale Brides Collection – all dresses styled to suit Ariels, Belles, Cinderellas and co. They're also the place to go if you want to give your white gown a twist: they pride themselves on their Dream in Colour range, where bodices, trains and hemlines come in 50 different shades to tie in with your colour scheme.

David's Bridal

David's have been tearing it up on the other side of the Atlantic for yonks – which is why we're so psyched they've finally touched down over here. You'll hear a lot of talk about these guys – names like Vera Wang and Zac Posen get bandied about since they've worked on 'affordable' collections with David's – but keep in mind that what's a bargain to your average platinum-card-waving follower of designer fashion doesn't always fit into that bracket for the rest of us.

I'll level with you: I've seen Vera Wang dresses here from £675 – no doubt more-than-nice workmanship if you can get it, and yes, a total steal if you're used to the £4,000 to £18,000 she's been known to charge. Last time I looked there were a few Wang gowns here under the £1,000-mark, but they also went up as high as £1,650, so you had to be careful not to have your bank balance stolen as well as your heart.

Mostly for £500-minus you're better off with the less name-droppy brands. Galina, for one: think elegant full-length gowns in modern-romantic styles—mostly strapless, often lace, always gorgeous. Then there's the signature David's Bridal Collection: trad-with-a-touch-of-something looks—the simpler the dress, the more likely to fall under our price range. DB studio are modern and daring – often going for the short or sophis markets – and I've seen prices start as low as £80. Last but not least, David's Bridal Woman is worth a look for sizes 18-30—expect plenty of flattering trad styles and occasional seriously cute retro-chic.

Ellis Bridals

Ellis have been going for more than 100 years, so there's no doubt they're doing something right. Again, you can expect a lot of classic cuts – A-line and fuller skirts, lace and sweethearts – but I've also seen them put out one or two quirkier styles, including a blush peach look and a Fifties rock 'n' roll hemline.

Eternity Bride

Quite a lot of classics here, but some simpler styles thrown into the pot, and a healthy dose of spectacle in black lace and inky blue numbers – plus, there's even a collection made especially for larger ladies. A real mixed bag, Eternity is likely to be a Marmite experience: some of their dresses will be the opposite of what you're after, and some you'll totally love – but it only takes one to get it right.

Impression Bridal

Fans of the ruffle, rejoice! Impression Bridal has them in all cuts, shapes and sizes. There are some slimmer gowns – think sheath with a sexy side split – but for the most part brides who aren't fans of froth need not apply.

Kitty & Dulcie
Magazine editors are constantly in awe of the price of these super-cute retro- and vintage-style gowns. The capsule collection of Fifties tea dresses and full-length lacy Twenties looks is too gorgeous to betray the price tag – which is generally around £250 and up.

Minna
Not only are Minna dresses a boho bride's dream come true – think swingy, loose, relaxed styles with lace and tiers, often long-sleeved or off-the-shoulder – they're by an award-winning designer who's often splashed across the pages of *Elle* and *Vogue, and* they're all ethical and sustainable. Not that you'd ever guess it to look at them – why aren't *all* dresses this heart-warming?

Are you ready for this? Gowns on the site have been known to go for as unbelievably little as… £155!

Pronovias
There's a real range of prices here, but as a baseline Pronovias bridal gowns tend to start around the £1,000 mark. For a showstopper that's closer to our £500 ideal, opt for their cocktail dresses in shades such as ivory, blush pink, peach and dusky purple. Expect a variety of styles and shapes that all ooze class and true glamour – think delicate sequin-and beadwork, simple satin belts and even striking modern ruffles, mostly in slim or swishy styles.

Pure Bridal
Pure's small selection covers most of the essential shapes and styles – skirts full and slender, hems above and below the knee, strapless, one-shoulder and halter – and yes, it does it simply and effectively. They even throw in a few wildcards with unusual colouring and appliqués, just for good measure.

Tobi Hannah

Tobi Hannah's standard collection is seriously retro cool – think knee-length Sixties shifts and Fifties tea dresses with a modern twist. But it's also that rare thing: a higher hemline at a bigger price – expect to pay about £1,200 to £1,800 a pop. Don't despair, though – the limited Alive! collection is talking our language: the short and tea length dresses are real one-offs, vary in size from 8 to 20 and are priced around just £600 to £800.

Best for: All sorts of wedding styles, but if you're a traditional ruffles-and-big-skirt bride in particular, I'd say this is the best route for you.

Sample Sales

If you really *have* to have a dress by a more expensive bridalwear designer, one way to save as much as 70% is in a sample sale. Most wedding shops have these a couple of times a year, when the dresses they stock for brides-to-be to try on are sold to make way for new collections – but some have ongoing samples for sale, so it's worth giving stockists of labels you love a quick call to find out.

Depending on the shop, you may need to sharpen your elbows at sale time – some offer appointments, many it's first come, first served, and occasionally it's a free-for-all – but you'll definitely need to be organised, patient and willing to be decisive.

The top tip I can give you? Turn up early. Bribe your maid of honour with coffee if you have to, but being first in line is the number one way to find *that* dress for hundreds of pounds less. They're sold as seen, on the spot, so if you're not at the front of the queue, every bride-to-be who turns up before you could walk away with your dream dress before you even get a look-in.

Bear in mind sizings, too. A lot of boutiques stock samples either in average sizes (10 to 14) or in large ones they can clip and tug smaller on each bride. Occasionally you'll find ones that sell sixes and eights, but they tend to be less common. While it might seem like a clever plan to buy big and have your dress slimmed down, some styles can lose shape and detailing if they're tailored too far. Your best bet? Ask the boutique owner before you buy – you might even be able to agree a price for her to fit it for you.

Best for: Brides who have fallen in love with a bridalwear designer who's out of their price range. Sample sales are especially good for brides of average or larger sizes, but it really depends on what the particular boutique stocks.

High-Street Bridalwear

It might not be as glamorous as a bridal boutique when you're trying on your wedding dress in the next fitting room to a girl pulling on a pair of jeans, but believe me, it's worth it – some of the high-street brands we know and love have gone to the trouble to design dresses that really are worth coveting.

I'll be straight with you: try on a £2,000 Ritva Westenius goddess gown and your high-street dress isn't going to feel as sumptuous. Meanwhile, if you're after full-on ruffle-mania you might even do better with a standard bridal boutique. But if you've set your sights on a fun, chic style that can be seriously elegant, since these labels often come in at less than £300, you really can't go wrong.

BHS

Styles are mostly simple and classic with a modern finish. In the past I've seen longer and fuller gowns at about £125 to £495, while shorter or simpler gowns – including a Pippa Middleton lookalike with cowl neck – have sold for around £80 to £175. And a little bird tells me you can expect even more affordable dresses from here on in…

Coast

We've all drooled over a Coast dress at one time or another, whether it was too expensive for the Christmas party or too elegant to go clubbing in. So why would anyone look down their nose at such a luxe brand when it comes to their wedding? I for one didn't – full disclosure: this is where I got my wedding dress from.

As you'd expect from a name with a fairly young following, there are those slightly higher-fashion details on these gowns compared to some of the others on our list – they got on board with the origami trend with a sheeny, structured bodice, and the high-front, low-back ruffle skirt has made an appearance, too. Expect to pay somewhere in the region of £115 to £695.

Debenhams

The Debut collection is a good call for empire line and sheath gowns especially, so if you're looking for something simple and classic – maybe with a high neck or lace cover-up – this could be the place for you. Prices from about £150 to £200 aren't uncommon, though there's the occasional £450-er. In the sale shorter styles have been known to go for as little as £35, and longer for less than £90.

Monsoon

Similarly to Coast, Monsoon is on the style pulse – one of their collections even featured not one, but two lilac gowns for the fashion-forward bride. Again, we're often talking sheaths and empires, so you'll want trad bridal labels for a fuller gown, but if elegantly understated is the name of the game, Monsoon has got to be a front-runner. Numbers-wise, think around £129 to £399 – but they have been known to do designs for as little as £85.

Phase Eight

On the whole another member of the sheaths and empires brigade, there's the odd slightly fuller or shorter skirt here – but the thing you'll get from Phase Eight is that little bit of extra embellishment. Tapework, lace and beading have all featured in their collections, and prices have ranged from about £130 to £750.

T.K. Maxx

There's been a lot of furore about T.K. Maxx launching a bridal-wear department – mostly because in true T.K. style they're not creating their own dresses, they're flogging designer ones on the cheap. To be clear, we're not talking Marc Jacobs or Vivienne Westwood here – the gowns are by a select few names with RRPs up to about the £2,545 bracket, and Maxx pricetags often between around £119.99 and £699.99.

In our price range, think dresses of the fuller, flouncier kind, with skirts running the gamut from ballgown to mermaid and A-line. They've also stocked the occasional dramatic twist in ruffled red, as well as slighter cuts with lacy sleeves and elaborate embellishment.

The labels? Look up Annais Bridal, Christian Wu, Dere Kiang, Donna Lee Designs, Hollywood Dreams, House of Wu, Jacquelin Exclusive, Sue Wong and Tracy Connop and you'll get the idea.

Best for: Mini-budget brides. In traditional wedding world, £500 is considered inexpensive for a bridal gown. In the real world, it's four or five times more than many of us have ever spent on a dress. Happily though, high-street bridalwear often comes in at under £300, with many shorter styles available for less than half that. And let's not forget: if you've got your eye on something more expensive, it can be worth hanging on for the frequent sales on some brands.

Bride or Bridesmaid?

Remember those gorgeous bridesmaid dresses you saw in that wedding magazine that turned out to be way over budget? I bet they're not more than you've pencilled in for *your* gown, are they? The thing with maids' dresses is that they *are* occasionwear – they're made with luxury and elegance in mind – but since very few people would pay more than a few hundred pounds per bridesmaid, they're rarely out of the realms of your bridal budget.

I'm not even suggesting you go for an offbeat colour if that's not your thing – there are lots of brands that offer their bridesmaid dresses in cream or white. And if you were looking for a simple, cute style anyway, why not save the pennies – after all, it's not like your guests will be any the wiser.

Here are a few fave bridesmaid brands whose gowns would make for some seriously chic brides – and since most styles are priced at around £100 to £200, they'll be pretty damn smug too...

Dessy

Simple elegance is what it's all about at Dessy: swingy chiffon column dresses that wouldn't look out of place on a far-flung beach, and slinky, sophisticated satin and charmeuse for understated glamour.

If you've got an unusual cut in mind – off-the-shoulder, cowl back or asymmetric neckline, for instance – there's a good chance you'll find it here, and the same goes for hard-to-get colours. Most gowns are available in ivory or white but if you're feeling crazy, some styles even come in polka dots and prints – and you can order 'extra length' versions if you're a taller Mrs-to-be.

Impression

Sheer overlays, ruffled necklines and hankie hems make Impression's bridesmaid range one to watch if you dare to be different on your big day. Many of their looks have a laidback prom or party feel, so if you're the type of bride who's known for bucking trends, partying 'til dawn and doing things your own way, this multi-tonal lot – most gowns are available in white – could be the collection for you.

Kelsey Rose

I admit it: I've had a thing for Kelsey Rose maids dresses for a while now. In fact, if you ask me, they're pretty much the height of bridesmaid chic. They're mostly modern, fitted and – dare I say it – even cool, with a few cute retro-inspired shorter skirts in the mix too. They're a smart bet for a range of necklines – strapless, one-shoulder, halter – and where ruffles do appear they're minimalist and finished with contemporary finesse. To top it all off, dresses come in an insane amount of colours, with most styles available in white, ivory and champagne for more trad brides.

Love By Enzoani

Enzoani regularly rock the bridesmaid world with their off-the-wall collections – we're talking *that* fierce embellished, coat-cut gown in magenta and their feather-light, breeze-catching daydream in lilac. If you're after a statement look like no other, this is the label for you – just bear in mind that for the most part you'll have to sacrifice shade for style: dresses often come in pastels and scene-stealing black, but I wouldn't set your heart on hard-to-come-by white.

Mori Lee

Their straight-up Bridesmaids collection is usually wall-to-wall floor-length satin and chiffon in sheaths, empires and columns. Most looks come in classic bridal colours and necklines go from romantic sweethearts to off-one-shoulders and halters – in short: floaty beach bride or city sophisticate.

Then there's the Affairs collection. Styles are normally shorter, lacier and on the whole go for a lot more of a 'fun and flirty' vibe, though you can also find versions of some of the Bridesmaids dresses here with hiked hemlines.

The Angelina Faccenda Bridesmaids collection is generally more like the first than the second – expect city-slicker classics along with a few pre-knee cuts, and more chances taken on the detailing side.

In all the Mori Lee collections though, be aware that the few taffeta dresses rarely come in whites, creams or ivories like the chiffon and satin do – instead, be prepared to compromise with something subtle like a gorgeously glowy champagne.

Best for: Barely-there-budget brides. If you haven't got time to wait for the sales on the high street and your numbers won't stretch much beyond £100 to £200, downsize your skirt and your outlay – then put your *actual* bridesmaids in a prettily styled, more low-key jersey number.

Surprisingly Doable Designer

Before I start on this one, let me say that these are *not* the only designer dresses I've got for you – there are lots of other options in a more strictly bridal style in the upcoming section – but I thought it was worth noting that if you're up for a not-so formal, unconventional get-together, there are both glam and laidback designer looks that are out there for less than you think.

Moschino Cheap and Chic

I'll be honest: the bridal possibilities here are few and far between – don't expect floor-length and be prepared to compromise on colour – but in the past I've seen a shimmering, cowl-neck, knee-length number that took the lame out of lamé for £509, while a pretty beige, lace look with waist bow made vintage-cute an affordable £407.

Proving beyond a doubt that the name's a total misnomer though, you're just as likely to find something in the straight-forward Moschino range – I once spotted a wrapover V-neck in creamy crepe for £509, and a pastel-pink ruched boatneck for £446.

Alternatively there's Love Moschino, where I've seen a registry office-perfect long-sleeve, funnel-neck jersey dress for £177, and a relaxed, white lamé-jersey dress with one short sleeve for £229.

Net-a-Porter

If you're willing to go as high with your hemline as your flavour of fashion, this online mecca could be a port of call. They *do* stock a bridal range, but unless you're ready for your credit card to take a battering, I'd steer clear.

Instead, take one of my top tips: narrow your search to dresses, click on the colours you're happy with – from white, neutral and silver to metallic, gold and pink – and arrange by price, from low to high. Then hold tight to resist temptation: be sure to only browse as far as your budget allows.

If you're after the all-out, floor-length white designer stunner, this isn't the way to get it (the next section is), but if you're looking for something low-key in a cute, Bradshaw-weds-Big registry-office number, this could be for you. The trick is to find the luxe not in the length but the fabric: that short, well-cut look in jersey won't do it, but in satin-trimmed lace you're indulgently casual-cute.

Not convinced? Here's some of the hot stuff I've found this way: Malene Birger had a cream, ruffled, mid-thigh lace number up for £310; Anna Sui debuted a daring long-sleeve mesh and satin look that was *not* for the faint-hearted – or strait-laced mothers-in-law – at £375; Alice + Olivia had me at 'hell*ooo*' with a slinky, beach-ready silk maxi for £395; Antik Batik went all ornate and elaborate in a silk blend with cheeky open back for £420; and there was a near-homage to Bradshaw in a Burberry London V-neck, high-shoulder style – just add sheeny bling – for £495.

Harrods and Selfridges are a similar story: more big names' short dresses in decadent fabrics for £500 and under. Apply the search technique and prepare for some serious knee wobbles!

J.Crew

Yes, some of their bridal gowns are more than £1,000, but if you're after a short or simply glam ivory style – think columns or sheaths in chiffon, silk or tulle – you'll still likely spot some picks around the £500-or-less mark. I for one was always a big fan of the floor-skimming boatneck, V-back Corrina and the slinky, square-neck, peekaboo Bettina. Littler brides – like me! – will also love the novelty of several styles actually being available in petite. Buy direct from their website (their wedding section is a *do* for once), or from the smaller selection over at Net-a-Porter.

Vivenne Westwood Anglomania
If you're dreaming of a white wedding, walk away now – Viv's statement, out-there Anglomania collection is for high-fashion brides with a kink in their style. I've seen a short-sleeved, knee-length purple number for £435 at Net-a-Porter, while a brocade-print piece with deceptively structured slouchy collar was £345. The collection can also be good for brides who favour the two-piece look – there was a time when you could supply the skirt and Westwood did a romantic red off-the-shoulder top to go with it for £300.

Diane von Furstenberg and Temperley occasionally have the odd short, white, lacy number for under £500, but for the most part the gorgeous gowns outside their out-of-reach bridal collection aren't so aisle-friendly.
Best for: Laidback, fashion-forward registry office dos. However gorgeous, these looks will get lost in a massive, high-ceilinged or cathedral-type venue, but they're just right in a more intimate setting, where they'll let your natural beauty do the talking.

The Designer Showstoppers
Here it is, ladies: exactly what I promised you back in the Basics section. You *can* walk down the aisle head-to-toe in catwalk names without breaking the bank, if you know where to look for them. And Here. They. Come.

THEOUTNET.COM
I actually can't get enough of this place. I just can't get over the gowns you can afford on there thanks to all this up-to-70%-off business. And since they're the sister site of Net-a-Porter too, you know they're on the level – not like some of those faceless so-called 'designer' online shops.

Many's the time I've daydreamed about festooning the super-simple Minimarket georgette maxi I once saw on there with some serious statement jewellery – not to mention stroking my laptop screen when I first saw the ankle-length Theyskens' Theory vision in silk that was only £146.

The cool Carven shell dress with twisted neckline for £189 would have been a head-turner at the registry office, too, while the not one but *four* Notte by Marchesa full-length gowns they had online at the same time – from only £322, by the way – would have owned any aisle.

Did I mention the Stella McCartney super-soft-pink lace dress for informal outdoor occasions? Or what about the crème de la crème for under £550: a long-sleeve, floor-gracing Amanda Wakeley silk-satin jaw-dropper? That, you'd just damn well build your wedding around.

But my favourite thing to do here? Take the tip from Net-a-Porter and skip the Wedding section in favour of searching by colour and style – the more open-minded the better. I mean let's be honest, if you're walking down the aisle in the grey Valentino Roma rosy-lace-smothered dress that was up for less than £600, the black Gianfranco Ferré V-neck that was under £550, the Vivienne Westwood black and blue jacquard-taffeta that was £525, or the red silk-organza and georgette Oscar de la Renta that was less than £515, who's going to blink if it's not white?

Saks Fifth Avenue
Busy brides, step aside. If you're going to order online from the States, you've got to have the time and money to send your gown back if it doesn't work out. Brides who are up to their eyes in work or other wedding preparations won't want to take the risk of being lumbered with a £500 dress they don't have time to post across the pond.

For those who do have the seconds to spare though, Saks Fifth Avenue have made a big hoo-ha out of the fact that they're now up for shipping worldwide. If you're after a short and simple dress, don't spend the international postage – there are generally styles similar to what Saks is hawking way more locally – but if you're struggling to find a longer look that suits your taste, the swish department store often stocks several standout options for under £500.

Example? Last time I checked, an Aidan Mattox with a beautiful curlicue-meets-sheer back was up for less than £315, while a seemingly simple cowl-neck ABS in satin revealed beautifully intricate silver and champagne back detailing – all for under £350. Meanwhile, the same brand's bow-detail strapless gown was textbook modern, origami-chic for under £250.

For glamour-hunters, there were various visions in gold – from Sue Wong's elaborately beaded and tightly ruffled chiffon number for under £445 to an utterly jaw-dropping gold V-neck, cowl back Notte by Marchesa stunner for under £430.

Also featured were a truckload of gorgeous, affordable BCBGMAXAZRIA, some glittering David Meisters and – if you've got just a little more to play with – a delicate, empire Badgley Mischka for under £610. There are even videos of a lot of the dresses so you can see them in floor-sweeping action before you order.

Shop Smart
There are just a few things to bear in mind when you shop online.

THEOUTNET.COM is an established, recognised brand, but there are a lot of cowboys out there hoping to fob you off with a counterfeit that crackles when you walk and costs your whole bridal budget – and possibly your sanity. Don't buy from sellers you haven't heard of, or who no-one you know has had positive first-hand experience with.

Always check the Ts and Cs when spending this amount of money on the web. You don't want to be stuck with a dress that doesn't fit because it turns out since it's sale stock you can't send it back.

You may need to get alterations, so you should factor these into the cost before deciding whether to keep your gown. Talk to an experienced, trustworthy seamstress or a bridal boutique that doesn't mind amending dresses other than their own before you decide it's the right dress for you.

If you're shopping from abroad, keep in mind extra charges – I've seen shipping priced at £9.99 and then taxes and duties tacked on at £80. It doesn't have to be a deal-breaker if you've laid eyes on your dream dress at a pinch-yourself price, but it's hardly pocket change so be careful to budget for it.

Best for: Brides with a lot of time on their hands. You have to be willing to wait for your dress to arrive, to get in touch with a seamstress for alterations, or to send it back if needs be. With discount sites like THEOUTNET.COM you've also got to keep an eye on Twitter or newsletters from your fave site so you can jump in and order your dream dress the minute it goes online – miss them and you could be left with slim pickings when it comes to choice of sizes.

Hire

No desire to wrap your W-day dress up in anti-moth paraphernalia and stash it in the attic? Or to try to convince your daughter she wants to wear it on her wedding day in 25 years or so? Go temporary and take all the savings that come with.

Go Local

I have a confession to make. For a while before my wedding I daydreamed about a little old lady – probably the cobbler from *The Elves and the Shoemaker*'s more competent other half – who would take in my dress for me, stitch on a few extra sequins and wipe a little tear from her eye in a grandmotherly way when I finally tried it on.

If that's the kind of experience you're after, you're not going to get it on the high street. Or at the jaw-dropping online hire place I'm about to wax lyrical about. But you might find it in that friendly neighbourhood bridal boutique I mentioned – as well as that warm, fuzzy feeling of supporting local biz (and not paying the earth for it).

Although hiring means it's likely your bridalwear choices will be more limited than if you bought – some fabrics can't be altered imperceptibly so they won't be available to rent – you will be able to add super-pretty prom dresses into the mix, and it's a way of wearing something heart-stopping that also keeps your bank balance the right side of red.

Wish Want Wear
Fans of Temperley, Badgley Mischka and Malene Birger, try to hold it together: gowns by these and other designers are available to hire online from Wish Want Wear – from as little as about £50. No, I haven't missed a nought off – last time I looked Birger-ites could hire a trim, super-cute style with cool, contemporary lace for four days for £50, or eight days for £85.

Meanwhile, Temperley lovers could get a stunning laser-cut, empire-line, floor-length number for four days for £165 or eight days for £315. Or even an embellished low-back look worth £3,835 for four days for £215 or eight for £415.

As for Mischka fans, you were looking at a totes-affordable £115 for a ruffle-loving halter neck for four days, or £215 for the same dream-dress for eight.

This is a site where it's worth checking out the wedding section (it's under Occasions, Bridal), but if you're open to other colours, you can also search gowns by names like Hervé Léger, Just Cavalli, M Missoni, MW Matthew Williamson, See by Chloe and co. according to everything from neckline to sleeve and body type.

Standout brides and designer addicts can hire their accessories here too – if you're into statement necklaces and eye-catching clutches, you can often rent names like Erickson Beamon for the price of buying a bling-tastic high-street gem. There are usually – for major label lusters – a few select Chanel by Vintage Heirloom quilted bags too, but you're unlikely to get them for much under £100, and they tend to be black.

The need-to-knows at the time of writing: delivery is available next-day, same-day and even on Saturdays; you can pre-book your delivery date in advance; minor spills and damage are covered; returns are free; they do the dry cleaning; they send you a free back-up size with your hire; and they offer a handy try-on service so you can test the fit of up to three dresses for £21.90.

I'd recommend calling up one of their style advisors before you book anything though – when it's your wedding, I can't help feeling it's best to confirm the availability of your date and size with a human being, rather than an online calendar.

Best for: Designer divas. Who cares if you don't get to keep the dress? There's no room in your cluttered loft anyway. My only hint: brides outside average sizes may struggle – there *are* gowns in sixes and 18s, but your choice will be more limited than your eights to 12s.

Couture

In bridal circles, this tends to mean going to one of the big-name couturiers and spending thousands of pounds having your dress designed and crafted to your exact spec. What I'm suggesting is a less intensive – and expensive – experience that's perfect if you've got a dream dress in your head that doesn't seem to be on the hangers.

I'll be honest: this option is going to take a lot of legwork. You'll have to Google/Yell.com/Thomson Local dressmakers or seamstresses in your local area, check their reviews online and call them up for prices. Numbers are likely to vary, but in general are cheaper for – you guessed it – shorter, simpler styles.

Your best bet is to ask around among friends and relatives – maybe even put up a post on Facebook or hit Twitter. You'll be surprised how many people have taken a prom dress to a tailor in the past or even know someone who makes clothes for a living. For me, working with someone who's been recommended by a pal you know and trust has got to be a better bet than hoping the reviews you read on that random website weren't just written by the shop itself.

Once you get down there, get to know your seamstress before you book anything. Ask to see samples of their previous work, or items they're working on now, and touch the fabric so you can see that it's of a suitable quality.

Then sit down and discuss their process – are they a one-man band expecting you to supply the silk, or a boutique ordering their fabric in at a range of prices? Make sure you get a written quote before they get started too – or you could end up having all the fun of bringing in cowboys to redo your kitchen and watching the price go up and up and up...

Best for: Brides of all shapes and sizes. Petite brides, in particular, might have trouble finding a style in your standard sizes, but as long as you're careful about the dressmaker you choose, this option could land you with a luxe, perfectly fitted look.

Charity and Vintage

More and more often, charity and vintage shops are taking on second-hand wedding dresses and selling them off at reasonable prices. If you're not worried that your dress has been worn once before and you want to make every penny you're spending on your big day count, helping out an independent vintage shop owner or the beneficiaries of a registered charity is the way forward.

Oxfam is really making a name for itself in the inboxes of wedding writers – and even if you can't pop into your local branch, their online shop is full to bursting. As you'd expect, there tends to be more in sizes 10 to 14 than any others, but new brides are giving over their gowns for a good cause every day, so it's worth checking back regularly.

To give you an idea, the most expensive dress I've seen them offer was a beaded, halterneck Johanna Hehir for £800, but really the majority of gowns have tended to go for less than £350. It's the place to go if you're after individual style *sans* the couturier too – with old-school looks from the Forties to the Seventies and unbranded pink and lacy confections, there's little chance of you getting copycatted by the time you walk down the aisle.

Best for: One-off brides. If today's gowns aren't making the right style statement, why not rifle through your local treasure trove and come out with something uniquely you?

CHAPTER 4

The Groom

Truss up your man without emptying his wallet

He might not make a big deal about what he wears normally – he might even be found lounging around in yesterday's joggers more often than not – but whether he says so or keeps it under his hat, there's a good chance your man wants to look just as ooh-la-la as you do on your big day. And even if he doesn't, I'd say the odds are *you* want him to – but in a hassle-free, less-than-expensive way? You've come to the right place.

Before You Start
Whoever you're trussing him up for, the same as with your dress, there are rules that can keep his costs down.

First up: two-piece versus three-piece. No prizes for guessing which of these costs less. So consider carefully before opting for a waistcoat that he'll only go and peel off at the reception anyway. If you really love the idea of a bit of extra colour, think along the lines of a more elaborately patterned shirt. Voilà! A dashing look that does less damage off the bat.

Second: single-breasted versus double-breasted. Double is a classic, but single is more modern – no-one will bat an eyelid if you send your groom down the aisle in a slim-lapelled, one-button jacket and skinny-fit trousers, *and* they tend to be less pricey. But if you're after a look that lasts, or that's more flattering for the larger lad, think about the double breast – just remember that most of the time, you're looking at a larger outlay.

Third: morning suits versus standard suits. Before you even get to the top hat, you'll find it costs more to put him in tails. Whether it's because of the formality, the quality, the bit of extra fabric or the fact they're harder to find, your average morning suit will usually push the numbers up. Plus, the big thing to consider here is that it's not just your man who's going to need one – just imagine him in his foot-high headgear next to ushers dressed like 007. Er, not so much.

Fourth: colour. It's not such an issue with your dress, especially if you're a trad-style bride, but considering his suit's colour before you buy could really help further down the line – especially if you're thinking of asking the lads to lug out their own suits if you can't afford to buy or hire theirs. In general, I'd stick to simple black – most guys who own a suit will own a black one – but the top trick is to talk to his best men beforehand and suss out a scheme that works for everyone. (More on that in the Bridesmaids & Best Men section).

Fifth: mix and match. There's no rule that says suits have to be the same shade from top to toe – or even the same fabric. If you're going for a laidback summer wedding, why not swap the heavy formalwear for yellow chinos, a crisp white shirt and a red linen blazer? If you're going semi-casual, you could even finish off the look with a cool, contemporary thin tie and Converse.

Alright, enough talk. Here they are: a selection of stops for everything from slim-line and subtle to patterned, off-the-wall suit styles, all via affordable morning suits in all their fancy finery. And I've tried to be kind: in most cases you can take home at least the jacket and trousers – if not the whole getup – for about £150 or less.

High-Street Hotness

A highly unscientific straw poll has proven without a doubt that when faced with finding places to look for our nearly-hubby's suit, most of us think of just two: Burton and Moss Bros. That's no bad thing – both offer options that are even better looking than their price tags – but I thought I'd save you some pavement pounding and outline *all* the best high-street bets.

ASDA

Yes, really – there's more wedding-worthy-wear here than you'd think. On the one hand, you've got their own formal trousers that have been known to go for less than £10 – and that's *full price*. On the other, there's their collaboration with none other than Mister Suit: Charlie Allen. The name might not mean as much as certain Fashion Week stalwarts', but the London couturier has been tailor-making swish suits in North London for more than 25 years – and his trousers for ASDA were just £20, jackets started at £45, and the most expensive formal coat was under £60 when I put pen to paper.

BHS

There's a surprising variety of shades and fabrics on the go at BHS. Yes, they're pretty standard, but I've seen jackets in greys, blues, black and browns and in fabrics from wool to twill and cord – all with the trousers to match. Shirts were simple, in shades from black and white to pastel blues, purples and pinks – though there are a few more patterns on the horizon. Back then I'd have said come here if he's an unfussy type with an eye for does-the-job basics, but I've since heard tell of a BHS black tie collection that's eminently affordable too...

Boden

When it comes to their suit jackets, the prices could make your eyes water – but if you've managed to keep the cost of the rest of the look low, they could be one to watch for shirts. The collared creations tend to be around £50 or less, and I've seen them range from simple white to neatly dotted full-on purple, chic slate to fun-loving rainbow-striped, and navy blue to grey with a cheeky print of London landmarks – a one-stop way to add some excitement to his attire.

Burton

Didn't I tell you you had good instincts? You can routinely get the full three-piece suit at Burton for less than £150. Trousers are generally around £40, as are suit jackets, with most waistcoats in the £20 to £45 bracket. They do regular, tailored and slim fits, and regular, long and short legs, so your man is even sorted at almost any size.

The palette here is primarily black, greys and blues, but you will find the odd brown shade if it works for you. Looks in the to-buy collection are generally contemporary, e.g. single-breasted, slim lapels, even statement chinos.

Don't forget their hireable range, though – here you'll find a lot more breadth, not to mention luxe. Curlicue waistcoats? You got it. Trad Highlandwear with kilt and sporran? It's all yours. More on that over in the Hire section, below.

Debenhams

The key thing here is not to be swayed by their made-to-measure service – ignore the signs unless you've got £500 burning a whole in your pocket. Instead, look for what Debenhams have long been good at: covetable collaborations with big-name designers.

Rocha.John Rocha generally gets my right-hand man's seal of approval, but the designer's suit styles are best caught when they're in the sale. J by Jasper Conran is a similar story – though in both cases shirts aren't out of the realms of affordability – but thankfully Debs is good at fairly regularly trimming much of its fashion's tags by up to 60%.

They're worth a sneak-peek for a good range of chinos too – in terms of colour, style and price – and as anyone who's ever set foot in a branch knows, there are always more shirts than you can shake a stick at, with many even available in 'big & tall' sizes. Go for Thomas Nash shirts for simple, slick colour that's often under £20, or upgrade to Rocha.John Rocha if he's more of a pattern or texture man. Alternatively, rent all his kit as you'll see below in the Hire section.

F&F at Tesco

As you'd expect from F&F, the look here is usually contemporary – less of the double-breasted and more of those skinny details that *Mad Men*-atics adore. Shades are largely in the grey area (ha, ha) but as usual black and blue tend to eke their way in. Prices are usually impressive – those less-than-£10 trousers are regulars – and there's sometimes the option to go for something with a sheen if it's his thing. They're also a good call for basic waistcoats – often under £20 – and for a tailored fit that doesn't push the price into the ether.

French Connection

I won't deny I'm caught in a bit of an FCUK obsession right now, so I'll hold my hands up: don't even window-shop if it's not sale time. When it is though, they do a sexy line in investment suit jackets – I've even seen single-breasted, 100% wool reduced to less than £50.

H&M

More realistic is H&M – an affordable menswear range that's even won over the hearts and minds of fashion eds at the luxury menswear mags. (I've seen you sneaking their coats, blazers and shirts in with the big boys' brands!)

H&M are known for their right-now style so expect your black, grey and blue blazers slender and single-breasted, and your chinos bright and daring (pink, anyone?). Shirts are seriously affordable and often have that extra bit of detailing – a black collar on a white shirt, maybe – that makes them the pretenders to the catwalks' throne.

House of Fraser

Beep, beep, beep! That's not me reversing – it's another sale-only alert I'm afraid. House of Fraser, God love 'Em, stock some suits that make you drool but, like a good-looking bad boy, can also make you cry. Keep an eye out for brands like Alexandre Savile Row and Ben Sherman, though, when 'tis the season to drop digits.

Jeff Banks

You'll only get the standard two-piece on-budget at Jeff Banks, but believe me, it'll be one worth keeping. Shades are largely a classic affair – grey, black, blue and the occasional cheeky check or pinstripe – and styles are a bit of both: look here for lapels' that range from skinny-cool to man's-man wide. They also do some shockingly good all-in offers from time to time.

Joules

I know, I know, another curveball – but bear with me. Suit makers they are not, but Joules know a thing or two about a shirt. You're looking at anything from £45 to £60 each in general, but for that you get the likes of two-tone cuffs and button-down collars when your groom sheds his jacket.

Mango

H.E. by Mango are another interesting call for shirts: from chambray to striped through gingham and check, they have the interesting touches you'd expect from their roundabout-£50 price range.

M&S

Savile Row Inspired one of their collections may be, but off-Savile Row pricing it is *not*. Instead, opt for Marks & Sparks's £99 looks

– you can usually get them in short, long, and one- to three-button, in the standard colour scale (you've probably spotted by now that that's from black to blue and grey to occasional brown). They're a good plan for shirts, too – at the time of writing most of their luxest numbers were under £40, and featured a range of both traditional manly and properly metro colours and patterns.

Next

They're not always at the cheapest end of our style scale, but there's something sturdy and reliable about a Next jacket. I say jacket because their premium suits are out of bounds, but you won't mind once you set eyes on their general collection.

In the past, for winter weddings they've done a gentlemanly tweed jacket complete with – eek! – professor-style elbow patches, and for summer they've been seen to showcase a lush-looking linen trio. Add one of their reasonably priced shirts – in all manner of patterns and shades, with those want-able tricksy details – as well as a pair of their coolly-coloured chinos, and your laidback, sunny celebration is well away.

River Island

Shocker, right? But the LOML (love of my life – sorry, I've always wanted to start an acronym) swears by River Island for style, comfort, quality and cost – and yes, enough so that he said his 'I do' in their clobber. And can you blame him? They're the best place on the high street I've found for a decently priced double-breasted blazer – a navy one for £70 has previously appeared on their racks, though they have been known to go up to as much as £110.

There's also a nice bit of variety in terms of shade and style – they've got your basics, but also a pop of stony colour, extra button or splash of piping here and there. My tip? Look beyond their standard suiting collection – it is super-chic, but their chancier blazers and shirts are where it's at.

Topman

It's Topman, so some of their stuff is classic, some is unusual, and some of it's raving-loony-out-there, if I'm honest. I'd recommend them if you're after a suit in an unconventional shade – previously berry, mustard, red and even insanely patterned blazers have all made an appearance – but be prepared that while many are doable, some may be fingers-crossed-for-the-sales prices.

They're also the place to be for shirts that could genuinely replace waistcoats – shiny, crazy-patterned and even leopard-collared have all graced their totally off-their-heads rails. If you're going for an alternative wedding that's all about celebrating your you-ness, on the high street, Topman really can't be beat.

Best for: Grooms who want to recycle their suit for work dos or other people's weddings, or who are that rare creature: the man who actually *wants* to try before he buys.

Hire

Let's be honest, there are parts of wedding planning that aren't really about practicality – there's too much romance and politics for that. So if he wants a suit he can hang in his wardrobe and stare at for the rest of his life, you can't really argue with him – after all, I'm guessing you've already got the protective bag and mothballs waiting in the wings for your little white number.

If he's less of the dewy-eyed type, he's after a look you can't afford or he just wants to feel the weight of luxury for a day or two, though, why not go ahead and hire his suit? It's a slick and savvy method that can save you some serious moolah.

There are bound to be plenty of boutique places right on your doorstep, and their prices will vary. If he's spied the suit of his Rat Pack fantasies in the window of the little place you drive by on the way to work every morning, I'd advocate calling up or popping in, talking pennies and supporting local biz.

But there are also places with branches all over the country – and this will help give you an idea of styles and prices versus other options, too. So here it is, my summary of some of the big dogs of men's formalwear rental, just for you.

1860 Suit Hire by Greenwoods

These guys have been handing out urbane outfits for more than 150 years, so they must be in somebody's good books. They've got the full spread: top hats and tails, DJs and bow ties, Argyll jackets and kilts – as well as all the trimmings, from waistcoats to ties to cufflinks. Mostly we're talking the typical colours and classic, wider-lapelled cuts, but there are a few surprises, like brocade grey or cream Prince Edward jackets. Roughly, prices start from £55 for full evening getup, £79 for the morningwear equivalent or £95 for the Highland outfit.

Austin Reed

Ah, remember this lot? The ones you always confuse with Moss Bros in your head – or is that just me? Well they've gone and got you the whole shebang and called it Q Hirewear. That's right: morningwear, eveningwear and Highlandwear that's mostly black, grey or navy, and favours the old-school look with lots of wide lapels, longer jackets and tailcoats.

The online outfit builder is a fun bit of kit – even if just for dressing up the model like one of those paper dolls you had when you were a kid – and you can pick from nearly 40 colours for the accoutrements to make sure he fits right in with your colour scheme. Price-wise you're looking at around £55 for eveningwear sets, £90 for morningwear packages or £75 for the full Highland look.

Burton

As I mentioned above, Burton is a good shot for suit hire. There's much more choice in their to-hire than their to-buy range and for the most part it's what you'd expect: classical W-day luxury that you can co-ordinate from jacket to waistcoat and tie to pocket square – plus a little Scottish spin with Prince Charlie jackets and sporrans if you're up for them. Try it out on their just-as-funny-as-Austin-Reed's outfit builder – trust me, you won't regret it. Prices are reasonable, too – think roughly £35 for an eveningwear package, £50 for two-piece formalwear and £70 for Highlandwear.

Debenhams

Can't wait for the department store powers-that-be to slash their prices before your big day? Or maybe he's got a man crush and won't tie the knot in anything less than a Jeff Banks? Either way, Debs's hire service could be the way to go. It's no surprise that they've got the lot – morningwear, eveningwear, Highlandwear – mostly in black and greys and the odd blue, and trimmed with the trad wider lapels.

If you're a morningwear fan, prepare to be tempted by the sheer number of styles: herringbone tailcoats, Prince Edwards, Panama Edwards that make it look like you're marrying Mr. Darcy – and I'm only just getting started. Prices start around the £35 mark for evening dress, £50 for morning suits, £90 for Highland packages and £57 for a little something from the man, Jeff Banks.

Moss Bros

Go on, nominate a Master of Ceremonies and make him wear the red toastmaster outfit from the Moss Bros Hire collection. *Pleeease.* Oh alright, but you can't blame me for trying – just wait 'til you see it.

There's more fun to be had in the shape of – you guessed it – morningwear, eveningwear and Highlandwear at Moss Bros. And you'd think so – they've had more than 160 years to sort out their closet. It's mostly greys, blues, black and – shocker – creams in those timeless styles, but you'll spot a couple of names you recognise in there too, like Ben Sherman and French Connection. Decent prices: expect to pay upwards of £38 for eveningwear, £55 for morningwear and £95 for Highlandwear.

Pronuptia

We all know where our local Pronuptia is – go on, close your eyes and you'll see it. They pop up everywhere you look and I'd bet the reason is that they're a franchise. That's also why when you Google the Parisian label you get about a million websites – so don't be fooled by the one in Strathclyde if you're a Midlander.

They've got our favourite three bases covered, but stock may vary by location – essentially, you're looking at styles trad and new, in shades from black to white and sheeny to matte. So yes, that means they're the place to go if your groom wants to pimp his suit – by which I mean say his vows in something like silver. Prices vary, but as a guide they seem to start from about £37.50.

Best for: Grooms who are an unusual shape or size – many hire shops offer a fitting service – or when you need to kit out the best men and dads too. Remember: a lot of them do 'groom goes free' deals when you hire so many suits, and it's also worth asking if you get your dress from a boutique that also does menswear hire – some will tack your groom on free if you're spending on your gown.

Online

Can't get him into a changing room, let alone a tailor's with the full tape-measure, awkward-in-seam-moment works? Buy the blokes' way – get him to browse the web on his favourite gadget and bookmark some looks he likes, then have them show up at your door for him to try.

ASOS

Oh, how I worship at the altar of ASOS. And you should too, if he's in the market for a cool, edgy number. I mean yes, they do your standard skinny black, blue, grey or brown suits and for the most part they're bang-on affordable – but it's the offbeat pieces that really make me drool all over my keyboard. I've seen them do white tux jackets, jade-green blazers – even a sumptuous navy velvet blazer. And don't even get me started on whole suits in suavé burgundy and indigo.

Tweed, herringbone, polywool – they've all been known to make an appearance. There's even been the full getup in grey stripes. And that's just their own collection – obviously they stock other high-street heroes too, like good old River Island.

MyTuxedo

On your average day, MyTuxedo's wardrobe pushes the £150 mark – you can usually get your morning suit for about a tenner over budget, but your choice is going to be limited. You're better off here for two things: statement waistcoats at reasonable prices – expect everything from Edwardian swirls and green tartan to red Victorian jacquard and seasonal novelty prints – and the MyTuxedo Outlet, where you can save as much as half the price on everything from bow ties and cummerbunds to two-piece suits.

Reiss Outlet

I admit it: even at their sale outlet a lot of Reiss suits are out of our price range. But there are also plenty of their largely standard-shaded classic-with-a-twist looks within it – and the range of wider as well as slimmer lapels mean they're a good bet for your more trad groom. One of the best looks I've run my eye over was a seriously strapping six-button, double-breasted grey pinstripe suit for £30 over budget – and I tell you what, I'd lose my tiara to see my man in that thing. But if your numbers are more rigid, don't lose heart: I've also spied a hot two-button, double-breasted two-piece for less than £130, not to mention several more sharp shirts that didn't cost the earth.

Very

The main thing to say here is don't let him just click 'suits' and say they're all too expensive. They pretty much are, if you do it that way. But Very is a site where it's worth doing the maths – pulling together a jacket and a pair of trousers he likes and checking they're not too wallet-stretching, rather than going for the pre-packaged, pre-whacked-up-price sets.

They usually have a good variety of jackets: in the standard colours plus the odd splash of interest in burgundy and co.; lapels wide and slim; fabrics sheeny and matte; details like piping and triple-buttoning and the odd surprisingly affordable double-breasted. Trousers tend to be a similar affair – and yes, they stock the unexpected shades to match the jackets – so all in all you're looking at classic-meets-contemporary looks with the odd offbeat update. And you can think of their shirts and waistcoats in exactly the same way.

Best for: Cool cats who can't find their particular brand of awesome at Topman, or changing-room haters who'd rather strut in front of their own bedroom mirror.

CHAPTER 5

Bridesmaids & Best Men

Your grown-up entourage gets gorgeous – on budget

There are all sorts of taboos about your best girls and boys that I hereby give you permission to ignore – and if anyone's got a problem with it, you can tell them to come and see me. Because back when your parents got married, the internet didn't exist – *that's* how many millions of years ago it was – so you can imagine that the rules on stuff like outfit colours, numbers and even who goes down the aisle first have changed (ahem: you or them, it's your call).

Before You Start
Believe me, I've had my head turned by many a bridesmaid brand. Remember my Kelsey Rose love from the Dress chapter? 'Nuff said. When it comes to kitting out the lads and ladies in your crew, it's your money and it's your call, but let me remind you of this before you and your groom appoint your aisle entourage: first, I'm guessing you weren't planning on spending the full £150 for your groom on his mates too, and second, it's not uncommon

for dresses by a lot of the big bridesmaid brands to cost £100 to £200 or more. Each.

Don't worry, that's just the smelling salts – it'll go away in a minute. In the meantime, how about we talk options that don't involve booting out all your bezzies?

Bring-Your-Own Bros and Bridesmaids

How many LBDs have you got hanging in the back of your wardrobe right now? And how many are about knee-length, without too-revealing a neckline? Most of us have got at least one look that fits the bill, and that includes your leading ladies. Since black is no longer a bad word in Wedding World, why not ask them to open up their closets in the name of love?

Have them come round with dresses that could do the trick and get their catwalk on in your living room, then once you've got it down to one dress each, look at creative ways of tying them together. Identical shoes or bouquets are one way to go if you can afford them, or a popular look that's worth capitalising on: pick a colour that fits your scheme and put a sash around their waists. The same thing *can* work if you've got your heart set on brighter BMs, too – trust me, daring to put everyone in different, complementary colours is the *height* of aisle cool.

And if it's good enough for your girls, it's good enough for his guys. Ask your partner in crime to check what colour suits his mates all have in common, then bring them over so you can suss out how best to co-ordinate them. You could ensure they all have a buttonhole that matches, but the easiest answer is to supply ties, socks and pocket squares (which, yes, are just fancy handkerchiefs).

Best for: Barely-there-budgets, mega-bridal parties (you have *seven* best friends!?) or last-minute nuptials. Who's got the time to get their own gown fitted, never mind getting all your girls and guys in one boutique?

Chip In, Chicks & Chaps

Weddings aren't the hush-hush, going-to-Daddy-cap-in-hand affair they might have been back in ye olden days – asking your girls and guys whether they want to chip in on their outfits is a normal part of planning. Don't worry: it's not scrounging and it's not out of order – it's a realistic chat that a lot of grooms- and brides-to-be – me included – have had at some point.

If you're planning to check out the chances though, do it individually. There's nothing worse than embarrassing the one friend who can't afford the cost any more than you can. Instead, catch them on their own, ask them nicely, and be sweet to them if they say no. If people start saying yes, gauge the kind of budget they want to spend and go with smallest number, or alternatively offer to top up the pot yourself.

There are a few things you've got to bear in mind if you go down this route though, and top of the list is that it's not for just-so brides who can't let go. If you know you won't be happy if their suits and dresses aren't exactly the way you want them, be prepared to dole out your own dough. Why? Because if they're paying for their outfits, it's only fair they should have more say, and get to go with looks they can wear again and again and again. Those flouncy pink ruffles you've been eyeing up recycled for your ladies' office Christmas party? I don't think so.

Best for: Mini budgets and low-maintenance brides – the girls get an excuse to buy a new outfit, the lads look dapper and you can afford a round of champers for the toasts.

Colour Me Happy

Whether it's you or them who ends up putting up the cash for your men's and maids' looks, I'm still black's biggest fan – trust me, no colour will give you more options in terms of brands or price range.

You can do what you want with it, too: add white sashes to your girls' black shifts for fun and funky Sixties monochrome, or come over all romantic with a statement diamante hairclip and pull off Thirties Deco.

Best for: Low-budget brides and silhouette-shy men and maids – way to flatter everyone, and treat them all without cutting out the cake!

Hire Their Handsome
I've already covered the top haunts for menswear hire back in the Groom section, so skip back that way if you're after the full rundown. For now, I'll sum up the forget-on-pain-of-death brands and budget tips to help maximise your money.

1860 Suit Hire by Greenwoods
Old-school dons of the industry who got into this racket more than a century ago, they still stock all sorts of classic cuts.

Austin Reed
Timeless meets modern thanks to trad looks and new technology, including their laugh-a-minute online outfit builder.

Burton
Some of the least pricey menswear hire I know, they've got your must-have W-day looks covered, and an outfit builder all of their own.

Debenhams
Your best bet for Highlandwear hire thanks to all manner of shades and styles, they also do the odd cool, contemporary borrowable by big boys like Jeff Banks.

Moss Bros
These gents have more than 160 years of history behind them, but that doesn't stop them stocking Ben Sherman and French

Connection next to their toastmaster togs, top hats and tails.

Pronuptia
Worth a pop if you're after something a little alternative, expect not only basic black and white but sheeny and surprising, too.

Best for: As I said back in Grooms, menswear hire works best if his mantourage is made up of unusual shapes or sizes, since many hire shops offer a fitting service. It's also a crafty plan if you need to kit out the best men and dads too, since a lot of hire places do 'groom goes free' deals when you hire so many suits. It's worth asking if you get your dress from a boutique that does menswear hire as well – as I said, some will stick your groom on free if you're spending on your gown.

A Fash in the Pan
If your girls are your style tribe – the ones you swap clothes with for a night out, and you shop with for a, well, Saturday – and you can't see yourself walking down the aisle without them looking just as wow as you do, there *are* ways to style them up, bigtime, without going for broke.

Local Biz
Remember the old lady in the bit about the Dress? No? Well, essentially I love to let you loose on local bridal boutiques. Most will offer certain styles to hire, but keep in mind that some fabrics aren't open to alterations and prices may vary. Whether you want to glam up your gang in beaded gowns, flirty Fifties prom dresses or something a little more sedate, your friendly neighbourhood wedding shop's wardrobe is a phone call away.

WishWantWear
How do your girls feel about floor-length, wine-red Badgley Mischka with an open, beaded back and cowl neck? Pretty damn

good, I would have thought. And how do *you* feel about only paying about £80 each for the privilege? Then believe it: WishWantWear just saved your W-day.

They stock designers from Halston Heritage to Hervé Leger, and M Missoni to MW Matthew Williamson. In our price range in the past? Floor-sweeping nude Malene Birger for £75, tea-length, flaming-hot pink, halter-neck Nicole Miller for £65 and bright red Tracy Reese covered with romantic petals for £50.

As I said back in bridalwear, at the time of writing the need-to-knows were these: delivery is available next-day, same-day and even on Saturdays; you can pre-book your delivery date in advance; minor spills and damage are covered; returns are free; they do the dry cleaning; they send you a free back-up size with your hire; and they offer a handy try-on service when you can test the fit of up to three dresses for only £21.90.

Girl Meets Dress

GMD are for-sure worth checking in with, especially if you're after matchy-matchy maids in unusual colours. If you're on the lookout for something strictly simple – like a jersey dress with a pretty front twist – look to their Butter By Nadia range, which has previously had you covered as of about £39 for shorter dresses, and £59 for something lengthier. There have also been plenty more unusual cuts among Gorgeous Couture's understated offering (mostly around £49 to £69 for two days), but don't be fooled if your girls are glamourpusses – there's plenty of glitz and ritz to come.

Scroll down the 'Bridesmaids' section underneath Occasions/ Wedding Boutique at the time of writing and you could find Dina Bar-El and Ruth Tarvydas having a grand old crack at aisle-gracing statement stunners for under £80, while if you were willing to go shorter you could get – deep breaths – purple, strapless Philosophy di Alberta Ferreti, no less, for £49. Elsewhere there was Marchesa Notte, Alice + Olivia and Halston Heritage under £60, not to mention Issa just inside £80.

A ... ecked, the necessaries here go ... on more than 30 days in adva... ek of your wedding it's free (the... insurance can be tacked on for ... ice; available rents are from two ... don't fit will be refunded; nex... re in the UK; and returns are ...

The...
The... section, if you're going to hire... one of their style advisors bef... ay, when it's your wedding, it's ... your date and sizes with a hu... calendar.

Be... ... hether it's you or your ladies wh... one way to be sure they'll wa... nfident smile.

Ta...
Wl... away. It's a tall order to get tr... r under £150 unless you're wi... ngs like fabric quality or fit. ... be done – I know a real-live br... ll sewn up for your besties is no... he same to you here as I did ba... ding the same info here and re... se I'm nice like that.

Best for: Maids of all shapes and sizes. If you're having trouble finding styles in your standard shops for, say, petite BMs, then as long as you're careful about the dressmaker you choose, this option could swathe them in an oh-so-spot-on fit.

Brands for Bridesmaids

If there's nothing for it, you just *have* to have off-the-rail looks for all your ladies, the usual rules of dress savings apply – namely, the shorter and simpler the style, the cheaper you're likely to find it.

Here's a roundup of some of my fave online and high-street heroines – I've done my darnedest to keep dresses under about £80 each wherever possible.

ASDA

If you're into the idea of your bridesmaids in black, then ASDA is a definite option. In the past I've seen a sweetheart dress with side frill and sheer panelling for £16 – *full price* – and that was just the tip of the iceberg. Lacy bodycons, curve-faking peplums or long-sleeved drapery – it's all been here for under £20. Don't get me wrong, this isn't the place for sumptuous silks and unusual shades, but if you're looking for something simple and classic, it's mini-budget bridesmaid heaven.

BHS

Outside the sales, you can expect classic bridesmaid looks to start around £60, and if you've got that kind of capital, it's worth a sneaky peek at their online dresses – they've been known to do web exclusives. Available in all kinds of colours – I've spied sapphire to fuchsia via purple and merlot – they regularly go right from size 6 to 22. If you can get your hands on the twist-and-wrap range, they can be strategically tied to make more than 15 styles – a smart shot if your girls are all shapes and sizes.

Otherwise, it's worth keeping in mind that they're a big stockist of Wallis, and you can often find their pretty, wedding-worthy looks for under £40. (More on this in the Wallis section, below.)

Coast

As much as I covet them, I'd recommend them at sale-time only, unless you're willing to shell out £85-plus per bridesmaid – but bear in mind that even then, a lot of the lower end of the price-scale is in black and jersey only. Outside sale time, you're looking at £100 or more for the silk and taffeta beauties we know and *sob* love.

Darling Clothes

These are a new one on me, but they're great for unusual-pretty. Think their elegant grey dress with tulip skirt and modern florals for under £50, or the green wrapover-bodice dress with three-quarter sleeves for less than £60. If you're after a feminine, vintage-inspired look that's ever-so-slightly quirky, the design-divas at Darling aren't about to disappoint.

Debenhams

An obvious choice for trad maids, Debs's own Debut dresses normally start at around £80, and go from short and sweetheart to all-out maxi. For something more affordable, shop in the sale unless Quiz is your kind of thing – by which I mean flirty chiffon and a healthy dose of embroidery or embellishment.

F&F at Tesco

It's F&F, so we both know it's going to be trés affordable – the upper limits of their dress range only tend to be about £60. It's worth a nod, then, that I've seen a few formal-enough contenders for even the classic bride's ceremony: a sheeny satin bandeau with brooch detail (£60), embellished halter maxis in black and blue (£40), an asymmetric purple prom dress (£35) and bow-front satin in four shades (£30) – and that's to say nothing of the black lace peplums and flower-embroidered knee-lengths if your do is lower key.

French Connection

I've said it before and I'll say it again: I'm a diehard French Connection fan, but outside the sales they're most likely to be big heartbreakers. That is, unless you're after something a little more casual – in summer I've picked up a sophis floral dress in jersey for under £60.

M&S
You know the first thing that comes to mind when you think of bridesmaid dresses? Those sheeny, trad looks are all over M&S. For longer classic gowns you're looking at around £99, while trimmer styles often start at about £69 – for which I've seen a pretty, understated little lace shift. They've also been known to do some seriously elegant options around the £75 mark – like wrapover V-necks that fall just above the knee and come in all sorts of colours.

Monsoon
There's only one reason to be in Monsoon, unless you're going on holiday (honeymoon kaftans, anyone?): they're the goddesses of elegant evening dresses that still work the now-factor. You can pick up the epitome of sophistication under £80 any day of the week – at the time of writing I had to hold myself back from an Asian-inspired wrap dress with chic floral print – but in the sale your nearest branch becomes a definite bridesmaid goldmine.

Examples: back in the day I spent a long time fantasising about following their Ophelia dress down the aisle – a blinding royal blue look, strategically boned and cut to just above the knee, I saw it back when it was reduced to £54 from £109. And don't even get me started on the ladylike lace all over the Cheryl, which was down from £139 to £69 – with that wine-red peeping through it was like 'hello, autumn "I do"s'.

Oasis
Like a bit of fun with your frock? There's plenty of it at Oasis, who've done brights, florals, hi-lo skirts and even jacquard-style patterns. But as well as the quirky, catwalk-esque one-offs, they do a decent line in simple class – and more often than not it's under £80 even at full price.

The kind of thing I mean: I've previously ogled a wine-red cowl dress with a double-take lace insert at the front and bigger at the back – it was sale time, so where it was originally £60, it had been reduced to £45, then again to £28.

River Island
RI have always been good at edge – I think of them for spiky platforms and fast fash – but these days there's also a surprising amount of W-day-able refinement. As long as you're not after anything serious and full-length, that is.

Naturally you're looking at a lot in go-to black, but lately it's their richly coloured range that really made me stop and look. A dark pink tulip dress with a pretty tie back? Seen it: £30. A sturdier light pink, lace-covered look? Spotted at £35. But what's got me right here over and over are their Limited Edition pretties – a merlot-coloured hi-lo hem with skinny belt has hit their hangers before for just £35.

Reiss Outlet
Non-sale Reiss is the kind of pricey that ruins days – heck, weeks! – but in-sale, seriously, it's the actual stuff of dreams. Their average of about £139+ has been known to plummet as low as the £40 region – and with everything from hot pink cowls to graphic V-necks and antique rose sweethearts, at the sale-time of writing I saw plenty of stunners all easily under £50.

Ted Baker
Like Reiss's estranged sibling, Ted Baker has a similar effect on me: outside the sale, we're out of its league, but in the sale, it's a real heart-stopper. Reduced to less than £80 in the past: a pretty-in-pink updated flapper (£75), sparkling gold high-neck with knot (£64) and lots of luscious black – sleeveless glamourama with gold-embellished shoulders was a personal fave (£75), as was a simple asymmetric number (£60) that I'd be tempted to never take off.

Very

Between Fearne Cotton and Holly Willoughby getting their mitts on the place and brands like Berkertex and Teatro touching down, Very is a veritable style melting pot. You don't even have to go up as far as £80 to get your maids their fashion fix – if you ask me, there's often a lot to love in the £65-and-under region.

Teatro have trotted out everything from draped nude satin (£65) to pencil dresses with subtle black lace (£65), via halters in flashes of hot pink (£65) and fun-loving embellished jacquard-print in jade (£59).

Berkertex (not to be confused with Berketex Brides) have brought what I'd call mother-of-the-bride (MOB) style for the most part, but they've still rocked the occasional more time-less gown. I've also seen a gorge rich-purple maxi with twinkly waist for £55, a monochrome strappy with swingy skirt and mesh corsage for £55, and a knot-front, cap-sleeve navy maxi down to £48.50 from £69.

In Fearne Cotton's corner, I've set eyes on a bright red, tightly pleated number with neon-pink sheer neck that actually looked like the most fun you could have with your gown on – and it was listed for just £59. I'm still a big fan of her one-time floor-length, cowl-back violet number, especially for beach weddings (£85), and the dare-you-to-be-different sheeny shirt-dress with sheer black overskirt (down from £59 to £17).

As for Holly Willoughby's collection, once found, the only way is up – except for the price, that is (hahaha, right?). Tipping the, erm, wallet, I've seen a purple, V-neck maxi at £69. Top of my wish-list: a cap-sleeve wrap dress in – ooh, black (£59); but if you're going low-key you couldn't go wrong with her red jersey cowl-neck (£39). I'd say think Holly, think fashionably ladylike.

Wallis

You've got to hand it to Wallis. Rarely do their occasion dresses top the £80 mark, but they've cultivated a definite rep for elegance. In the past I've gone gaga for their black, purple and floral numbers in everything from twinkly knee-lengths (£40) to ruched high-necks (£40) via my best in show: purple printed with white flowers and delicate gold birds (I'm seeing a pattern here... £40). For the sheer number of wedding- and budget-appropriate looks, if you've only got time for one high-street stop before your big day, I'd nominate this one.

Warehouse

The classic maids' look this is not, but if you're after a little something more fashion-ified, walk Warehouse's way. They've previously done jewel-shouldered shifts for £45, while sheer florals and nude wrap dresses have caught my eye at £25. The main shade here – as with any high-street brand – tends towards the all-round flattering black, in which I've seen everything from Deco embellishment (£30) to don't-look-now-Nan sexy peplums (£40).

Best for: No fuss, no muss. Get your bridal dress fittings to yourself and only have to draft in your maids from all corners of the earth on one day – or even ask them to try on the same dress at their respective branches without hopping on the train. Wham, bam, dressed you ma'ams.

Brands for Best Men

Lo and behold, another hot topic I've already hit up – check back in the Groom section for all the ins and outs. Otherwise, here's a skinny-as edit of all the most crucial content when it comes to best men's brands.

ASDA

One of the cheapest menswear options, they also stock style from an unexpected source: an affordable collection by Charlie Allen, suit-smart London couturier.

ASOS

The last word in cool, contemporary edge, expect ASOS's slick collection to cover everything from skinny lapels to risky blazers in tweed and velvet.

BHS

After your standard black, blue or brown suit with understated shirt? BHS is a boon for basics. Check out their totes-affordable black tie range, too.

Boden

Stop here for shirts only, and pick from patterns and prints in a sophisticated style.

Burton

Great prices as ever, Burton covers the three main '-wears': morning, evening and Highland. Choose from regular, tailored or slim fits.

Debenhams

Worth a look-see at sale time, they're the home of Jasper Conran and Rocha.John Rocha. Shirts are a steal at any time of year.

F&F at Tesco

Bag a bargain in the shape of contemporary cuts and tailored fits. They're also tops for waistcoats with mini price tags.

French Connection

Investment pieces all. Walk this way at sale time only.

H&M

The suiting label high-fashion mag eds can't believe they love, they're the ones to watch for that dash more detailing for your dollar.

House of Fraser

I can resist anything but temptation. Stay away outside sale time or watch your wallet wilt under Alexandre Savile Row and Ben Sherman.

Jeff Banks

Built to last, looks range from classic to contemporary and plain to pinstripe. Surprisingly good offers on full outfits come and go.

Joules

Head here for shirts with that little something extra.

Mango

Another scene-stealer in the shirt arena, they add their own stamp to make your best men stand out.

M&S

Stick to their £99-and-under suiting, and shirts spanning simple to something else.

MyTuxedo

Head-turning waistcoats in heritage styles + the MyTuxedo Outlet for suits and accoutrements with half off = this place is one to watch.

Next

Go along for jackets with a twist – think elbow patches or light-weight linen.

Reiss Outlet

The den of double-breasted choice is at the higher end of our spend scale, but worth casting an eye over for a longer-lasting look. Prepare for a mix of old and new styles and single-breasted suits, too.

River Island

My other half's pick for style, comfort, quality and cost, expect everything from straightforward suiting to some of the best double-breasteds on the high street – not to mention a few offbeat offerings.

Topman

Topman is as Topman does: sometimes it's in the mood to be suave and snappy, others it's the high street's village crackpot. Try it on for everything from smart suits to loony shirts.

Very

Pick your own pairings at Very – it's worth the extra legwork for splashes of unusual colour and contemporary details.

Best for: As I said back in Grooms, high-street suits are good for guys who want to recycle their suit for work dos or other people's weddings, or for that rare creature: the man who actually *wants* to try before he buys. They're also a good bet if you're asking your boys to foot the bill.

CHAPTER 6

Pageboys & Flower Girls

Turn them into little angels for heavenly prices

Beware: if there's a baby-loving bone in your body, you're about to get broody. I'm not a mama, but I imagine one of the funnest things about having a mini-me is getting to play dress-up with your little lad or lady. Now *you* get to do it like the fairy-princess auntie, dishing out tiny suits and dresses in your big white gown and then giving the kids back to their parents when they need any actual, y'know, parenting. And thanks to my totally magic tips, you can do it all for £50 or less per squeezable punum. You can thank me later.

Before You Start
If your wedding's diddies aren't your own, talk to Mum first about whether there's a smart suit or pretty party dress that she can rake out for them. If that's not an option, before you go down the hire road or buy road, make sure you check any special style requirements. The last thing you want is tears on the day because Peter's skin is sensitive to wool or Nancy's never liked yellow.

Best for: Fussy little misters and misses (and their mums and dads), or tinies who aren't over the 'I can dress myself!' stage.

Brands for Tiny Togs
Brace for cute-pact.

Alex and Alexa
Keep in mind this is a place that sells Dolce & Gabbana for little 'uns – prices can go up to more than £300 for a gown. But if you're determined to dress your living dolls in something downright gorgeous, it's worth waiting it out and stopping by during sale season.

At the sale-time of writing, my fave picks for girls were a Torres turquoise velvet dress with rose detailing, down from £67 to £46.50; a simple La Stupenderia pink and white dress with old-school frilly collar that was reduced from £151 to £45; and a Kickle beige high-neck dress with velvet polka-dot waistband and hem, cut from £68 to £34. For boys there was less that appealed within our price range, but a Tom & Drew navy blazer – down from £62 to £31 – was worth a second look.

Sizes range from newborn right up to 16 years-plus.

ASDA
ASDA's childrenswear might not be what you'd call tailor-made for weddings, but it's worth working your way through the rails when dresses start from as little as £4 or £5. You're unlikely to find your classic white or ruffled, flouncy prettiness here, but I've spied floral pinafores with leggings (£10) and pretty prints such as butterflies (£8) and birds (£5) that would be super-sweet for colourful summer weddings.

There's more here for boys if you're after the classic W-day look, but I'd recommend starting in the school uniform section. Usually their simple, short-sleeved shirts start from about £2 or £3 for a two-pack, or longer sleeves go from about £3.50 to £4.50 per pair here. I've seen trousers start from £3 – even including a brown option – and it's regularly £10 or £11 for a straightforward boys' school blazer.

Sizes start at nine months, and go up to around age 18.

Belle & Boo

They're at the more expensive end of our scale, so avoid outside of sale time if you were looking to spend less than £40 – not least because the super-cute animation on their homepage will reel you right in. Made for girls only, this is the place for very vintage-inspired style – dresses will remind you of picture books your nan used to read to you. What do I mean? Last time I looked I fell for a faded-blue dress with tri-colour buttons and an old-fashioned carousel print at the hem (£44).

Sizes tend to range from 18 months to six years.

BHS

There's a good chance the pretty looks you put them in won't outlast sticky fingers, drinks and cakes, so why spend more than the roughly £30-plus you'll get teeny occasion dresses for at BHS? If you can't find what you're looking for in-branch, check the website, where they've been known to hide some exclusive colour-ways.

The most expensive dresses I've seen for tots under 18 months here were £40, going up to about £60 for 12- to 14-year-olds. As always, BHS is a good one for traditional basics – for littler ladies, that's looks like dainty white shifts with bouffant netting, and coloured underskirts with girlie butterfly sashes. From age two up, I've seen the big girl's equivalent with room for more flowers, as well as reams of extra white-on-white and even lace-covered options. You can also expect romantic, lacy looks in all kinds of colours, as well as a mini version of the adult maids' twist-and-wrap range.

Mini-men's outfits start from around £30 for a waistcoat, cravat, trouser and shirt set, or I've seen them from about £38 for a simple black, four-piece suit. Waistcoats tend towards the trad swirly style, but you can expect them in everything from ivory to dusky pink – or you can pick up plainer styles but they are likely to be less cost-clever. If you're struggling for a tiny tailcoat, they've been known to have them here from £35.

Sizes generally range from six months to 16 years.

Château de Sable

Remember smocks? Or those little velvet Peter Pan-collar dresses you never believe you used to wear when your mum brings them down from the attic? They're really good at all that old-timey stuff over at CdS.

For boys, the fact you have to buy his shirt, jacket and trousers as separates makes them out of our price range – you can expect to pay around £29.99 for shirts, £32.99 for trousers and £69.99 for the occasional blazer.

For girls, though, we're talking velvet dresses with little bows on (£34.99) or high-necks with pleated skirts (£39.99) – and I've seen those yes-you-really-did smocks for about £43.99 or £44.99. But the real bridal-pleaser? They often have little ladies' styles in white – so you're sorted whatever your scheme.

Sizes go from newborn through to 12 years old.

Childrensalon

If you thought Alex and Alexa was pricey, wait 'til you check out this little baby – Dior for £536, anyone? Well it *was* reduced from £765. Over in the real world (that's £50 or less, remember?), the girls get a fair bit of dress-up stuff, so you're all set if you were imagining a diddy Cinders sprinkling petals to the altar. Other than that, they tend towards daintily patterned smocks and pastel colour-block dresses – except at sale time, when you might snap up a heart-printed Hucklebones London number (down from £72 to £50) or properly antique-style red-velvet Darcy Brown with tulle underskirt (was £67, down to £47).

For little boys, choice is more limited – it's the bugbear of having to buy several pieces – but in the past, the Boutique Brands label has offered a shirt, waistcoat, cravat and trouser set for one- to 12-year-olds for £39 full price, while for nought- to 7-year-olds, they regularly offer a five-piece tux for about £50. At sale-time, their three-piece jacket, waistcoat and trouser sets for 11- to 15-year-olds have been known to fall from £59.95 to £41.95 and their two-pieces from £62 to £20.

In a nutshell: come any day for ye olde, or keep your fingers crossed for the new in sale season. Sizes? From zero to 16 years.

F&F at Tesco

I'm going to come right out and say it: these are the cheapest trad-style flower girl dresses I've found in my travels, and when they're going to grow out of them in no time anyway, you don't need to go bigger-budget.

Type in 'bridesmaid' on the website and at the time of writing you'd get a simple, high-neck, embroidered white dress for all of £18, an A-line white one with rosebud neckline for £25, or if you really wanted to go all-out, a delicate mesh-skirted number with satin sash and detachable corsage – just £37. Sizes generally range from firstborn to nine or 10 years.

Don't type in 'pageboy' – you'll get nothing. Split it in half and last time I looked 'page boy' brought up everything from a two-piece white linen suit for £27 to a blue cotton waistcoat from £9, matching trousers from £12 and jacket to top it all off from £24. These are usually for five- to 14-year-olds – for really mini misters aged three to six you're looking at the likes of a four-piece tux set for £31.

Gap Kids

GK deals mostly in low-key looks, so don't expect to find anything too trad here. It's on the cost-effective side – which we *like* – but only if you're looking for the likes of simple heart-print and ruffles (£14.95), neon lace tanks (£19.95) or floral-print satin (£22.95) for girls over five, or pink tulle with a sailboat print (£17.95), pink with a navy, scalloped top (£17.95) or a tiered tulle ombre dress (£19.95) for five-year-old ladies and younger.

Outfits for boys under five are mostly too casual for your aisle, while for four- to 13-year-olds shirts tended towards the £14.95 to £17.95 region. Check under schoolwear for trousers in shades from stone to black (about £15.95) and the occasional twill blazer in greys and blues (£32.95 – though I've seen them reduced to £25).

John Lewis

Ah, *Jean Louis*, as we call it in our house, on the grounds of it being so ooh-la-la fancy. And yes, they've been known to sell Nicki Macfarlane pink silk that tots up to a whole £125 of our hard-earned cash money. But as long as you stick to girls' partywear – since their bridesmaids' dresses are often £55-plus – there can be some pretty little savers to be had here.

In the past I've been a big fan of their own-make blue, pink and cream floral high-neck for two- to four-year-olds – yes, it was reduced to £18, but even at full price it had only ever been £26. Root around if you're in the market for pretty flower prints and embellished-to-the-hilt little sparklers, but only pick up your standard white-with-a-sash-type dresses in sale time.

John Lewis Boy suits are often a happier story: mostly navy with the odd hint of grey or black, I've seen waistcoats at about £16 to £18, jackets £35 to £38 and trousers £18 to £20. Admittedly that stretches ever-so-slightly outside our price range, but it's not unfathomable if you're only after a two-piece, or you're just after the jacket to top the trousers.

Sizes are mostly for two to 13 or 14 years, but there are styles for newborns up to 12 months.

Joules

You won't find trad white looks for little girls here, but what you will get at Joules is a little bit of elegance for tiny types. At the time of writing, their totally kid-friendly wrap dresses were my personal favourites – from tartan with a sash to red with dainty flowers or white with a pretty pink pattern, you could just see your flower girls twirling around with smiles all over their faces (£37.95, but reduced to £24.95 in the sale). For lower-key days, they generally do a nice line in colourful dresses printed with flowers and the like as well (often around £24.95 to £44.95; again, cheaper at sale time).

For snappy little sirs, you're usually best off sticking to their shirts – and only if you want to add some pizzazz to their existing suit. Usually around £27.95, they're not cheap, so only turn to them if you're after specific styles, like quirky blue and red gingham or colourful checks.

There's a little bit for baby ones, but most styles are for three to 12 years.

Little Duckling

Getting hitched under exposed beams in a barn, or down on the farm? Or maybe you're going for a countrified or historic, Medieval feel? You've probably guessed by now that Little Duckling is pretty one-off – simple, old-school shapes for the super-old-school bride.

Girls' dress styles tend towards the just-under-£40 mark for the most part, but have been known to go for half that during the sales. Expect lots of block colours and the occasional check pattern in loose, practical, nightie-type fits and long-sleeve dresses.

Boyswear mostly matches the girlswear – perfect for that aw-aren't-they-a-pair moment – but again this stuff is far from formal. Forget jackets and shirts and think jersey pants with knee patches (down from £23.50 to £11.75 in the sale), as well as the odd pair of linen trousers in neutrals or brights (were £31.95, reduced to £15.98).

Sizes bridge the gap from new babies to seven years.

Littlewoods

If you like BHS's prices but can't find your perfect style, Littlewoods are a good alternative in about the same ballpark. For girls, expect plenty of trad cutesie white with pretty little details, as well as the usual prom styles in nude or brighter colours. Expect their costliest occasion dresses for girls aged five and over to be around the £55 to £65 mark; I've seen an ankle-length, sheeny white look with a sprinkle of beads on the bodice at a just-beyond-budget £54, and a pretty pink tulle number with front and back waist bow for £62. They've also done looks with bejewelled waistbands (£54), embroidered bodices (£48) and organza stripes (£36).

For boys, blazers and jackets are few and far between, but the ones that have popped up in the past included a two-button black or blue number from £12 (reduced from £24) and a fully lined pinstripe by Taylor & Reece for £35 – tweed, meanwhile, can go up into the £40s. A four-piece grey suit by Ladybird came out at £32-plus for the waistcoat, trousers, shirt and tie, while the three-piece beige version (*sans* tie) started from £26. There's always the option to go through the schoolwear too, where you're looking at around £8-and-up for two-packs of trousers.

Sizes vary per style from as young as newborn right up to 16 years old.

Matalan

You can say 'ba-bye!' to classic white over at Matalan, but there are often some pretty party looks that could make the cut. All sorts of styles are regularly under £20, and have been known to range from bright pink pleats with a sequinned waistband (£18) to a couple of Candy Couture skater dresses with lace overlay: one in rosy pink (£16), and one in cream (down to £8 from £16).

When it comes to the boys, if you're going for a laidback day, they often do a decent line in kids' coloured skinny jeans or chinos (I've seen them from about £7 or £8), but for a high-class affair there are also sometimes a few more formal pieces. Itty-bitty gents' black or grey suit trousers usually start at about £8 to £10, matching jackets at around £22 to £25, and shirt and waistcoat sets at roughly £10 to £12 – in the right season they've even stocked them in silver, black, dark purple and deep red.

Sizes vary by style but can go from newborn right up to 16 years.

Monsoon

As you'd expect, Monsoon don't let us down in the style stakes – there are plenty of pretty, fussy white things you're about to fall in love with. Just be careful to check the tags before you let the littlies into the changing rooms – while most dresses are under £50, there can be a handful in the £55 to £120 range.

Among Monsoon's rails I've seen some of my favourite flower-girl looks of the whole high street: a soft purple dress with white net skirt and white lace overlaid on the bodice (£48); one with white net skirt, draped cap sleeves and what can only be described as a doily-style top (£40); and a white, short-sleeved dress with rows of corsages along the chest, each with a tiny, five-leafed golden centre (£50). *Sigh*.

Little lads aren't left out either – suits with jackets are usually out of our price range, but there should be plenty of simple, stylish four-piece sets with trousers, shirt, tie and waistcoat around the £40 to £50 mark, as well as understated waistcoat, shirt and tie sets – no swirls in sight – from about £28. A standout fave for me, though, is a look I once spied for slightly offbeat weddings: a red and grey checked shirt, red tie and grey deconstructed, knitted waistcoat from £26.

Sizes mostly go from zero to about 12 or 13 years old.

Mothercare

Red velvet and that little girl smile… It's back to colour and fun again at Mothercare. Most dresses are casual enough to get your little girl confused with a lost child as she wanders down the aisle, but there is the odd party dress that could have your colour scheme all sewn up.

At the sale-time of writing, under-threes could step out in oh-so-autumnal feather print (£25 to £26), bright pink with sequins (£10 to £10.50) or a velvety fabric in teal, purple or red (£13 to £13.50, £19 down to £9.50 and £14 down to £9.50 respectively). As for girls up to 10 years old, their closet included a pastel pink high-neck with sequins (down from £22 to £11), a bright red number with sequinned bodice (down from £22 to £15) or purple poly-mix taffeta – with a flowered waistband (cut from £16 to £11). Girlswear sizes tended to go from about nought to 10 years.

Boys' shirts are often impressively affordable – think chambray and brushed cotton almost always £10 and under. Trousers can be more of the cords and chinos ilk, but are mostly £10 and under too, and the one shirt, tie and waistcoat set I found last time I checked was down from £14 to £6. Blazers were quirky and retro and under £20, including a stripy BabyK with heart turn-ups and a Little Birds by Jools striped number in faded blue, brown and cream. Sizes for boyswear tended to be in the nought to 10 years range.

myCinnamonGirl (and boy!)

There's a very vintage vibe to myCinnamonGirl – just looking at the ruched, elasticated bodices will give you back-in-the-day flashbacks. Think green, frilly-hemmed and floral dresses (down from £39 to £19.50 in the sale) or soft-pink tulle ballerina skirts (reduced from £29 to £21.75) – the perfect fit if you're going for an afternoon-tea theme of wild flowers in jam jars and charity-shop china, but not so much if you prefer to stick to the traditional side of the garden path. Most prices are around the £29 to £49 mark, though those can drop down dramatically in the sales – I've seen £49 dresses reduced to £8.82.

The capsule boys' collection can be found via the dropdown menu on the left of their site, and though mostly casual, it can include some cute and quirky old-school touches. In the past I've loved a little tan waistcoat (down from £27 to £20.25) and a super-sweet double-breasted knitted cardi with teeny-weeny elbow patches (cut from £39 to £29.25). Altogether now: 'awww!'

Girls' and boys' sizes have been known to span from 12 months to 11 years.

Next

I've daydreamed about having children *just* so I can put them in Next clothes – I mean, look at all the cute characters, pretty prints and luxe embroidery. In girlswear for the under-sixes there's been a pastel pink dress with flower print for £9 to £10 and tiers of florals and ribbon for £22 to £24. Then there was the crossover collection for three- to 16-year-olds with its dark purple ruffles for £40 to £47, pink asymmetric dress with flowers along one shoulder for £28 to £35 and candy pink scene-stealer with a Peter Pan collar and sequinned bows at the hem for £36 to £40.

For boys under six, smart styles for a low-key summer wedding have included chinos in shades from grey to hot pink for £9 to £10 paired with plain, checked or striped shirts at around £8 to £13. Then there was the crossover suit collection for one- to 16-year-olds: trousers and waistcoats started at around £15 and slim-lapelled jackets – in grey, black or cobalt – began at about £30.

If it's a deft mishmash of fashion and formality you want, I'd say Next is your brand.

Vertbaudet

Here's a statistic that's actually worth hearing: at the time of writing, 100% of the dresses at Vertbaudet were under £35 – most under £29 – and that's *not* in the sale. They've done a white and dusky-pink party dress with scalloped hem (£29), a light pink dress with bow print and cream waistband (£29) and a blue dress with a voile overlayer and black appliqué ribbon flowers at the neckline (you guessed it, £29). As long as you're happy with block colours and the occasional print, there are plenty of looks to choose from – often with pretty under-netting and surprisingly swish fabrics.

It's a similar tale in their boyswear collection, where sweet, sunny shirt-and-shorts sets including a white poplin top with bib and beige or grey shorts have appeared at just – ooh – £29. And their cute little jacket with elbow patch and crest? Erm, yes, £29. Trousers are often on the even lighter side of your pocket – available in grey or black, I've seen the simple, regular-fit pairs as low as an iddy-biddy £9, and regularly around £13. You'll need to do a teensy bit of trawling to pluck them out of the ether, but at such tidgy prices, they're totally worth the work.

Sizes normally go from newborns to 14-year-olds.

Best for: Kitting out the teenies without all the tantrums – pick up in-store or order online and drop off to Mum without once manhandling a child into a fitting room or getting them to sit still for a tailor. *And* relax.

CHAPTER 7

Shoes & Accessories

Put your best foot forward, but don't pay top dollar

Dylan Moran says women have no feelings. His explanation? 'Because it's actually men, you'll find, who are far more romantic. Men are the people you will hear saying 'I've found somebody. She's amazing. If I don't get to be with this person, I'm *beep*. I can't carry on. I mean it – she's totally transformed my life. I have a job, I have a flat, it means nothing. I can't stand it, I have to be with her, because if I don't I'll end up in some bedsit, I'll be alcoholic, I'll have itchy trousers – I can't walk the streets anymore.' His point: 'That is how women feel about shoes.'

Yes, Moran is a comic genius. But apart from that, he proves something I've long suspected, despite not being so much of a 'shoe' girl myself (tops are my thing – you can never have too many tops, and they go with *everything*): it doesn't matter how long your dress is; how many metres of train your 50 bridesmaids end up hefting down the aisle behind you; that you'll be kicking off your heels the minute you stumble into the bridal suite. You're *still* going to what something utterly

81

stunning under your five layers of petticoat. Because *you'll* know they're there.

And you – and he – will get it. For less than £100. Oh, and then some shiny new accessories – clutch, cover-up, jewellery, undies, veil, the whole shebang – on top. 'Cause I'm nice like that.

Before You Start

Step away from the Louboutins. I know, I know, you love them to a point of obsession that us non-shoe-girls may never understand. But unless it's sale time at Selfridges those secret sparklers could cost you your band. Just put them down, so I can help you. Because what's in a name? Especially when you've got that bottle of red nail polish…

Lust-Have Brands

Not convinced? Fair enough, but if you *have* to have designer treads, at least make sure you Choos them wisely (ha, ha). First up: shop in the sale, plain and simple. A pair of new-season catwalkers can easily cost you upwards of £500, whereas mid-season discounts can slash the cost by as much as half.

Second: shop at THEOUTNET.COM. I know, I know, I've said it before, but they're my go-to site for cut-price quality. I've watched a pair of DKNY silver T-bars with floral detail go for £58, down from £130. Strappy nude Diane von Furstenbergs? £88 from £250.

Colour

Which brings me to my next point: white, as we've ascertained, isn't as abundant as your oh-so-chic common or garden black. Whether you're hunting down designer or you're happiest in high street, don't be afraid to come over all noir and your options will open right up.

Alternatively, if you've got a fave pair of shoes already – mine are the glitter-smothered red Dorothy platforms I was wearing when I met the man at the end of my rainbow – forget the shade and slip your pinkies right into them on your big day. After all, who cares if they're not white? You and him will be the only ones who know they're there…

Bespoke Touches
I'll level with you: unless you're magically bezzies with a shoe designer (in which case, get out: you have a responsibility to the rest of us to get yourself some totally free foot-stompers), I'm afraid, ladies, bespoke toe-togs just aren't gonna happen.

But that doesn't mean you can't add the personal touch – and I'm *not* talking getting your craft on. Sure, a few strategically glued Swarovskis couldn't hurt (unless you let my co-ordination-free fingers at them), but a quicker, simpler, and some might say chicer way forward is a pretty pair of shoe clips: beautifully designed accessories that simply clamp right onto your plain heels. Art Deco glamour, blousy flowers and romantic hearts, here we come!

Shoes
If you're less captivated by label lust and more by style seduction, here come my favourite brands for getting some serious works of art under those arches – whether they're yours or your groom's – as well as sandals, shoes or dress-up clips.

Ladies' Only
Here come the girls… In shoes made by brands that love us and us alone.

Coast
Coast exist purely to serve your special occasions – which is why they know exactly what we want in a big-day shoe. Styles are regularly between £65 and £100, and have included suede with toe caps that resembled rose-gold mesh (£100), as well as simple lace-covered point-toes (£75) and finally strappy T-bars with cheeky neon tubing (£80).

Dorothy Perkins

I once had a pair of DP flats that lasted 365 days despite being worn for at least 10 hours on all of them (I told you: not a shoe girl) – and that's why I'm pointing these ladies out if you're looking for footwear that's built to last. It's not unusual for their heels to start from a teeny-tiny £19 – for £23 I've seen black or nude courts with sheeny-pretty toe caps. My fave bridal style of, well, ever? Their nude peep-toe courts with backs and heels covered in gold glitter. Needless to say, they're the place to be whether you're after sleek and simple or footsie-fashionista.

Elegant Steps

Be still, your beating heart if you happen to be a trad bride. Whether it's the classic pointed toe with satiny bow or a little bit of round pearling or twinkle, you're likely to find it at Elegant Steps from about the £29.95 to £39.95 mark – full-price. But that's not all: the multi-brand stockist also happens to have itself a collection of stunning shoe clips that I've seen start from £14.99, or even £10 at sale time. Expect to pick from the likes of diamante or sheeny coloured bows, Art Deco crystals and even little pompoms.

Irregular Choice

Irregular Choice, of course, do exactly what they say on the tin: footwear so deliciously nutty that you can't get it out of your head. I toyed with a pair of their crochet-covered white shoe-boots with flowered lining for my W-day, but ended up settling on those glitzy red heels I mentioned – a whole lot less bizarre, but no less extraordinary (to me, anyway).

Don't come with a mind to find anything that isn't utterly crazy – as I write this, a pair of bright red platform boots with *a doll on them* and what I'm pretty sure is the mushroom from *Super Mario Bros.* is staring at me – but know that when you do find them, shoe girls for miles around will flock to you *just* to fall at your feet. And how could they not, when the shoes have names like Gravitational Pull?

Top of my list for my-eyes-are-up-*here*-not-on-my-toes moments were, at the time of writing: the Park Lanes – woven white mid-heels with an abundance of pink and white faux flowers on top (£99.99); Flick Flack, with their intricate Eastern-style pattern in silver and fluffy fold-over white upper (£79.99); and We Found Love, not only for the name, but for the wacky curved shape, shimmering heel and autumnal bouquet on the toe (were £89.99, reduced to £55 in the sale).

Littleblackdress.co.uk

If it's an entrance you want, it's the unabashedly statement slip-ons at Little Black Dress you get. I've seen some to-die-for diamante kittens here down from £45.95 to £25.95 in the sale, but in general you can pick up their pretties between about £40 and £300. Sticking to the sensible side of that bracket, expect the likes of diamante-smothered Moda in Pelle marchers for £89.95, or glitter-covered gold Aftershock London Jolies for £76.

Monsoon

You know how much I love their wedding dress collection? Well, let's just say they've got the footwear to match. I've found a simple patent, nude court shoe for £59 before, but at the same time over in their bridal section you could bet on everything from flat white pumps with Deco flower detailing for £55 to high-heel satin peep-toes with sparkling oval brooch for £75. *Swoon!*

Moda in Pelle

Littleblackdress fans, come right to the source at the bridal section of Moda in Pelle – and expect eye-popping shoe-candy that won't be quickly forgotten. At full price, the bridal collection's RRP tends to range from about £39.95 to £129.95 – and I've seen them touch on styles from covered white platforms with big spangly trims to subtle gladiators sprinkled with swirling sparkle (beach big-day, anyone?).

Miss Selfridge

For the most part, Miss S's shoe style tends to swing between fashion and fierce. Bridal may not be their base, but you can look to them for so-now touches fit for romantic, gothic or offbeat brides. First up, in the past I've spotted nude, laser-cut shoe-boots in lace-like (£46) and flowery styles (also £46). For biker brides, nude and black peep-toes studded with don't-mess spikes were £65. And for unusual types, nude 'Western' courts with suede platforms, gold trim and cowboy-boot-style patterning were £65 too.

Nelly.com

They might not strictly have a bridal department, but that doesn't mean there isn't plenty of wedding-worthy 'wear over at Nelly. com. As well as your simple white, plain heels, think high-fashion mimicry at high-street moolah: at the time of writing I was loving ruffled platforms for £45.95, strappies with Eastern-inspired gold-circle embellishment for £46.95, ankle-strapped stilettos with cream top and sugar-pink bottom for £46.95 and fearsome platform boots with zip back and that 'cushioned' or 'pillowy' leather-look panel that makes you think of vintage Chanel handbags. Truly scrumptious.

Topshop

Topshop's trademark is their so-now, so-hot luxe for less, and trust me, when it comes to W-day they won't disappoint. Don't expect your traditional white-with-diamantes here: opt for the likes of nude-top, black-bottom platforms (£55), peep-toe mid-highs with golden glitter on heels and soles (£62) or chunky black platforms with intricate cream, laser-cut panels (£80) and Make. Your. Mark.

Wallis

Classy ladies, walk into Wallis, where it's all about simple polish. Colour-wise you're looking more at nude and silver than white, though you might be lucky enough to stumble across a cream. Shapes? I've seen ballerinas with angular metal bows (£28), courts with finely stitched knots (£29.50) and sleek nude wedges (£35).

Unisex

Off on a his 'n' hers shopping spree? (Well, they're the shoes, not The Dress!) Pay some attention to these men's *and* women's labels and get the pair of you togged up in top toes.

BHS

Trust me: give BHS a go. You might surprise yourself. Because they sure-as surprised me at the time of writing with their mega range of bridal toe-warmers. They started from £22 for ballerinas with bows or the traditional glitzy round brooch, before going on to strappy sandals including gold-sequinned kitten heels for £26, right the way through bow-trimmed courts (£35), appliqué-flowered peep toes (£40) and diamante-embellished platforms (£55).

For the man in your life, there were the likes of trad black slip-ons (£19), pointy-toed formals (£28), tan loafers (£38) and crinked brown leather pointies (£38) in the mix.

Debenhams

I hadn't heard of Jenny Packham before I got entrenched in Wedding World, but it turns out she makes a living designing red-carpet dresses for A-listers. Which is why I'm just a *little* bit excited about her affordable collection of everything from shoes to headgear for good old Debs: No.1 Jenny Packham. Styles have included white satin peep-toes with crochet detailing (£85) and elegant point-toed, translucent lace slingbacks (£55).

Elsewhere at Big D, their in-house Debut collection covers covetable styles in a rough price range of £18 to £48. They're mostly classics with a twist – I've seen ivory slingbacks with a diamante bow (£28), their simpler knotted, ruffled counterpart (£32) or lace-covered kittens (£36).

Meanwhile, grooms have their hands full with all kinds of traditional and classic-meets-modern shoes: I've spotted Thomas Nash slip-ons for £30, Red Herring lace-ups for £50 and Jeff Banks designer treads for £65. You can't go wrong.

Dune

All that glitters is at Dune. If you're no diamante diva, turn on your heels now – if, however, you're a glamourpuss, it's time to kick yours off. Why? Because this is the place where the wedding range has included everything from silver, reptile-print slingbacks with jock-off diamantes (£85) to Deco-influenced twinklers in soft gold (£99).

Men who dare to be different would be in their element here too – last time I checked, simple black lace-ups and slip-ons were nigh-on equalled in number by off-kilter looks like anaconda-print, tasselled loafers (£99), slightly less bonkers ombre brown brogues (£85), duo-tone brown lace-ups (£85) and pinstripe-patterned deep brown shoes (£89).

Next

Love, love, *love* their women's cream occasionwear shoes because they're Next doing what Next does best: styles that somehow manage to be modern and classic, all at the same time. Take the 3D floral courts with ankle strap that I eyed-up for a long while: they were all trad-peep-toe-meets-new-platform, and the timeless flowers were freshly appliquéd with subtle loops of sequins (£45). There were even matching ballerinas for the all-important first-dance moment (£38), or simple, ivory Mary Jane peep-toes for minimalist chic – or brides who see shoe clips in their future (£28).

On the men's side, I for one have raised an eyebrow at the cheapness of their black panel lace-ups – 'Only £25? Am I in the right shop?' – but the truth really *was* that good. And that wasn't the end of it, either. Expect brown slip-ons around the same price, as well as classic wing-cap brogues – many shapes are often also available in different shades and slightly more luxe finishes as around £30, £45 and £48-plus versions. The tasselled loafer has even crept in around the £50 marker, if he's so-inclined.

New Look

So it turns out New Look have gone and got themselves some friends in high places. Narrow their footwear collection to cream, white and silver styles on their website and at the time of writing they came up with everything from Moda in Pelle glamourama – i.e. textured silver platforms (£69.99) – to Pink London glitter strappies (£59.99) and – *chokes on cuppa* – even Irregular Choice mid-heels topped with a blousy white flower (£74.99).

But it's not just the outsiders who were bringing the fashion credentials to this party: their own-brand lace-covered white courts with ankle straps (£29.99) and white crochet sandals with dainty gold-ball detailing (£24.99) would look right at home on any aisle.

There were touches of big-fashion, little-price genius among their men's clodhoppers too: burgundy, washed leather-look lace-ups were a quirky take on trad men's formalwear for £24.99, and basic pumps got an upgrade with leather-like black tops for £12.99. For grooms with more classic appetites, there were plenty of leather-look loafers and side-lacers under £25 – just don't expect to find the real stuff on their shelves.

Office

I'll say one thing for Office: they give good sole. Especially if you're after something edgy, high-fashion or alternative. Not so much your traditional, elegant or understated shoe – for that you're better off with one of the brands above – but for daring brides I've seen white mesh and crochet pumps (£25), dizzyingly high white platforms (£75) and quirky and oh-*so*-cool white leather jazz shoes (go on, I dare you – they were only £55). How can you say no?

Expect your man's head to be turned too – his favourite brogues went mid-green or burgundy suede at one point (and they were by a brand called 'Ask the missus' – er, no need!) for £69.99 – in amongst all manner of loafers and lace-ups that were mostly under £80. If he's the kind of chancer who might risk gold glitter on the day though, maybe don't let him go in unsupervised (no, really – I saw them with my own eyes for £71.99)...

River Island

Kapow! Your River Island footwear has arrived – and that means so have you. Never ones to do things by halves, I've been sucker-punched by everything from white studded lace-up brogues (yes, we're still in the ladies' section, and they were £35) to chunky wedges plastered in buckles (£60), sexy peep-toe, stiletto ankle boots (£80) and – oh yeah – lovely pointy courts (£50).

As for the men's: no mock-leather here, just the good stuff from a tidy – sorry, *tiny* – £30 a shot. If he's one for texture, your nearly-HB would have had his eye on the light-brown backstraps as soon as he walked in the door (£34.99), while shiny-types would have honed in on the black leather pointy-toes (£39.99). After a compromise for your trainer-addicted casual Casanova? I just have to say this: there was a time you could literally make it a pair of – uh-huh-huh – blue suede shoes (you heard the man!) with contrasting yellow and tan soles (£40).

Sarenza.co.uk

I've honestly never seen so many white heels in one place – so if you're looking for options in the shade of the season, Sarenza is worth a watch. I've pored over chic, sheeny mid-heels with a neat toe-knot (£86), point-toes with pearl embellishment (£106.70), kitten peep-toes with bow and teeny laser-cut effect (£119) and wave upon wave of simple white sling-backs.

As for *Mr* Missus, it's been refreshing to see a groom's shoes section. Packed in-between the seemingly endless onslaught of classic black lace-ups, there've been jump-out-at-yous like dapper white Derbys (£79.90), grey nubuck lace-ups with blue treads (£87) and ombre light-brown leathers (£84.15).

Schuh

I never really thought of Schuh as being off their rocker – and indeed, I have found clean, white point-toes here for £60 – but what struck me most at the time of writing was the barrage of totally mental footlockers, like white brogues heeled on a ginormous black, serrated sole (once £55, I saw them plummet to £14.99 in sale time). Besides those, though, there have been some doable-with-your-head-screwed-on styles, such as low-heeled Hush Puppies with three sweet straps and heart cut-outs all around the trim (£60) and a vintage-lovers' dream: cream woven shoe-boots with green and beige layered bows at the back, which strutted out of their Irregular Choice shoebox for £75.

For men there's the usual menagerie of loafers, slip-ons and tassels mostly in black and browns, but sneaked in among them I have spotted just a few bonkers strokes of genius: tan leather moccasins that were just this side of serious (£55), lazy, dark-brown leather espadrilles (£55), navy boat shoes with white laces (£60) and, oh yeah – *pewter* Dr. Martens with the kind of sheen that blinds you (£54.99), or cowboy-style shoe boots with just a little engraving of one scantily-clad lady on the upper (gratefully a not-in-this-world £170).

Men's

He might get away with his Converse if you're going for a super-cool, models-off-duty style of day. If you're after the romantic, sweep-you-off-your-feet kind? No worries: these guys have gotcha.

ASOS

I know, I know, they do ladies' too, but it's not often so bridal-friendly, unless you happen to be jonesing for strappy silver. You'll find that happens a lot in this section, but I know you've got the stones to make it through.

As you might imagine from the ever-on-trend model-types at ASOS, there's more here than meets the well-trained, loafer/tassel/lace-up-seeking eye. That's not to say there isn't the usual – it's here in medium-sized spades – but I've also found brown, blue and grey (this is *one* shoe) brogues with white and orange soles (£40), grey suede Derbys (£35), grey *leather* Derbys (£42), black leather Derbys with trio-tone sole (£45) and, ahem, velvettasselledloafers. Sorry, that's: dark blue, leather-soled, velvet tasselled loafers (£50). *Whoa.*

Burtons

Ah, Burtons: good, safe, bloke-friendly fun. Point him in this direction and send him off on his merry way, job done. Because how can he go wrong with brogues, loafers and round-toes in shades of black, brown, grey and burgundy, textures from shiny through matte and sometimes even crinkly, brands including Ben Sherman, and prices that are regularly safely in the £28 to £55 bracket? *And* breathe.

Clarks

Trust Clarks to do a solid line in classic and modern men's shoes – even if one or two of them look like they should be on little lads' feet (I'm looking at you, Velcro fasteners). As well as the usual crop of black-and-browns – mostly with what looks like seriously supportive soles – I've spied on-the-pulse but not off-their-head possibilities: creamy-coloured lace-ups with white soles (£49.99), two-tone Oxford wing-tip brogues in brown and tan (£99.99 *wipes brow*), cognac leather brogues with white soles (£69.99) and navy leather semi-casuals with white piping (£59.99).

John Lewis

It can take some self-restraint to go men's shoe shopping in John Lewis – there'll be many a tongue-lolling moment that turns out to cost over our odds – but it's worth it for the treasures he could well turn up. Some of my fave finds on past sprees – ahem, browses – included Ted Baker dark or light-blue suede brogues (£100), walnut, high-grade leather boat shoes (£89), navy leather boat shoes (£65) and Bertie patterned, off-white leather Brogues with that deliberately dishevelled look and blue innards (£75).

Topman
I wouldn't expect anything less from those bright young things at Topshop than the hotchpotch collection of classic and cavalier looks they stocked at the time of writing. Most exciting: bright red brogues (£80), brown lace-ups with gold corner-detailing on the upper (£65), black suede slip-ons with studded heel and collar (£65) and granddad pointies covered heel-to-toe in herringbone (£65).

Jewellery
Prepare for a magpie moment: what I lack in shoe-wareness I make up for in a thing for all that's bling. So whether you're in the market for sparkle, shine, colour, cocktail or the real deal, here's my pick of places to swoop in and nab something special for your W-day nest – as always, for less.

Accessorize
I know this one's on your high-street radar, and so it should be – its range of beautiful things has earnt Accessorize its rightful place at the top of my lust-have, can-have jewellery pile. Their gorgeous Wedding Accessories collection (that's right!) has been seen full to bursting with creamy pearls and Deco designs, from short-drop pearly clusters (£4) and ovals of diamantes with pearls (£7) to silvery heart-on-heart bracelets with crystal detailing (£12) and a simple pearlescent ball wrapped in strings of silver (£12). And that's before we've veered off into the white lace cut-off gloves (£9). *Ohhh* yeah...

Azuni London

Azuni is about gold and colour, colour and gold – at the time of writing, it was a place for turquoise bracelets with exotic influences (£45), woven cord friendship bracelets (which I saw reduced from £55 to £22.50) and super-thin, textured, semi-precious-stone rings (£35). Wear with saris, Alfred Angelo's Dream in Colour dresses or anything that could take a touch of magic from far-off lands.

Bouton

Last I looked, Sparkly Bouton were all about faking it to make it in clean, modern styles. Couldn't afford that giant pear-shaped diamond? Swap in a rock of CZ was £95. No ruby earrings in your price range? Make it round, brilliant-cut red crystals was £75. Admittedly the prices of necklaces and bracelets aren't so charming – some can be in the £300 range – but Bouton's a bright and shiny way to top up what you could afford of the real thing. And it's not all costume: their styles are set in sheeny sterling silver, no less.

Glitzy Secrets

Sparkle, anyone? After all, that's what good old Glitzy does best. Wedding fashion photographers love the label – it never looks out of place next to their £5,000 dresses – and you'll soon see why: pearl and diamante earrings aplenty have been known to start from just £12 full-price, while necklaces have taken off around the £14-mark and bracelets from £15. For that I've seen everything from Forties-style pearl-cluster bracelets like Nanna used to wear (£15) to modern collisions of silver hearts and round sparklers (pendant, £15) and even old-Hollywood pearl clip-ons for piercing-free prettiness (£14).

Karin Andréasson

Karin's creations are at the loftier end of our penny-scale, but the not-impossible trinkets are often a touch of fairy-tale elegance. Imagine these past beauties: a thin gold ring in the shape of a bended key (£52), the dainty 'kiss a toad' ring with said silver amphibian on top (£65) or my personal favourite, if after all this saving you have the spends going spare: the Love Spy necklace, with a pair of silvery binoculars that could be pulled up the length of the chain to reveal two tiny, dangling hearts (£82).

Monsoon
I bring this up because it's an oft-forgotten fact that all Monsoon's accessories are not in fact over at Accessorize. Admittedly, their little merry-go-round of in-shop boxes aren't quite as purse-loving as their counterpart's collection, but there have been some truly beautiful pieces to make it worth your while – like a doubly-strung pearl bracelet topped with an intricate silver and diamante brooch (£25) and a pair of pearl drop earrings with statement Deco pear-drops that I wore to my best friend's wedding (£19).

Oasis
I've been keeping close tabs on Oasis's jewels for a while – their lashings of cream and pink and ever-feminine styles have made them a hot pick for brides for seasons and seasons now. I've lusted after their enamel flower bracelet – three entwined tiers of white blooms, each inset with a teeny diamante (£14); the stone-stretch bracelet with five look-at-me layers of dusky diamantes, creamy, pearly rounds and chunky, rosy rectangles (£14); the golden heart collar-clips strung together for a modern twist to high necks (£8); and the sparkle pearl collar – reams of the stuff for an elaborate finish as required (£16).

Oliver Bonas
Damn do I love the jewellery at Oliver Bonas. And not just because I've seen necklaces start at £8, bracelets start at £3.50 and earrings start at £4.50 either. It's because I can't get enough of their classic-meets-modern-meets-vintage styling – not to mention the fact that a lot of their silver stuff is *actual* 925.

I mean, last time I was there you were looking at everything from just-interesting-enough triple-oval silver drop earrings (£12.50) to a super-cute golden merry-go-round necklace (£18) via the delicate silver 'key to my heart' bracelet (£19) – with heart-topped key, if you were wondering – and look-at-me elaborate 18-carat gold-plated oval and pearl necklace (£28). Need an affordable answer to your bridal-jewellery prayers, pronto? These guys are all over it.

Olivier Laudus

Classic brides in search of pearls, nature lovers hunting leaves and flowers, and colour fans after a pop of glamour – all of you will find your look in one fell swoop among Olivier Laudus's matching bridal sets. At the time of writing, prices started at £29.99 for necklace and earrings together, while elsewhere, necklaces began with strings of pearls at £24.99, earrings with pearl and crystal drops at £14.99 and bracelets with pearls and hearts at £23.99.

Among my standouts: the Thalia wedding bracelet – a golden mesh of circles and diamantes with a boho, vintage vibe (£24.99); the Abigail Pearl pendant – a deep drop of silver, rhodium, CZ and pearls with a Grandma's-jewellery-box feel (£35.99); and the Camilla chandelier earrings – elaborate twists and leaves of sparkling Swarovski crystal (£39.99).

Tatty Devine

A treasure trove for quirky, colourful and retro brides, at the time of writing, Tatty Devine had all the bright red hearts in diamante crowns (necklace, £21) and tattoo-style love hearts with 'bride' and 'love' sashes that a girl could ever wish for (necklaces, also £21). Way to add an instant flash of fun to your nowhere-near-traditional day.

Tebi Jewels

As they love to point out (and wouldn't you just?), Tebi have graced the pages of *Elle*, *Vogue*, *Stylist*, *Cosmo*, *Tatler* and *More!*

magazines. So if you ever needed convincing that they know their fashion, consider yourself well and truly told.

Nature, far-off lands and brilliant colour have all been themes – think gold-disc earrings printed with trees ($20, about £13), magenta spheres with tails of golden chain ($12, about £8) and unmissable bibs of turquoise and gold ($36, about £23). Just be aware that, ordering direct, you're looking at postage of around $23 – about £14 – and a minimum wait of about 1 to 2 weeks. The lesson here? Don't order too late, and do order all you need in one sitting.

Topshop

Another one that's been under my watchful gaze (I just couldn't help myself), Topshop have a higher-than-expected hit-rate of bridal bling – especially if you happen to be near their mega-shop on London Oxford Street. Prove it, you say? At the time of writing, there was exhibit A: edgy, diamond-shaped earrings of gold chain and diamantes, £14; B: beaded white stretch bracelet with delicate blush-pink rose, £5; C: stack of floral, diamante and bow rings in shades of gold, cream, white and pink, £12.50; and D: catseye charm stretch bracelet adorned with rose, leaf and crystals, £7.50. Case. Closed.

Yarwood-White

Try the lovely Yarwood-White for a touch of bridal boho – just make sure you stick to necklaces, earrings and hairpins if you don't want to veer off the budgetary track. If you're a fan of laidback-chic designers like Temperley, Delphine Manivet and Matthew Williamson, you'd have given in to the temptation of these gorgeous looks I've spotted so far: a fern-leaf-style drop necklace of diamante and real ivory freshwater pearls (£60); pink Swarovski crystal and peardrop smoky quartz earrings (£40); or a cluster of pearls and diamantes arranged as per a flower at the tip of dainty hair grip (£20).

Wish Want Wear

If nothing but the biggest names will do but your pockets aren't as deep as your label-love, it's time for another trip to Wish Want Wear. They don't do their jewellery by halves round these parts though, so don't come looking for anything dainty or delicate – it's big, bold, here-I-am glamour all the way.

My picks of the blingin' bunch to date: a whacking great Badgley Mischka crystal bib necklace (£40 hire, £600 RRP) and an Erickson Beamon crystal and onyx chunk o' hunk: all fat twists of creamy pearls, gothic black chains and rainbow Dovima crystal (£50 hire, £1,005 RRP). Talk about the definition of glamour.

NB: Check out my Dress section and the Wish Want Wear website for deets of WWW's hire policy.

Ziba Collection

Take a walk on the wild side at eclectic boho-zone Ziba Collection. Between the gold filigree and crystal chandelier earrings (£30), tear-drop pendant with freshwater pearl, pink quartz and royal symbol (£25) and the cream multi-row strings of pearls with modern, diamante-tinged spacers (£35), at the time of writing it was the place to add a handful of something-specials to your dreamy, laidback look.

More, More, More: Skip to the Rings chapter for more gorgeous jewellers for every big-day budget – and bridal style.

Clutches & Cover-Ups

Who cares if it's windy or the temp goes sub-zero? In cover-ups like these, let it snow, let it snow, let it snow. As for our got-to-have-it gadgets, they'll be tucked away in the comfort of the perfect bridal clutch.

Accessorize

Here we go again – but Accessorize never gets old. They're too on-the-fashion-pulse to ever let that happen. Their wedding bags collection (yes, that's actually what it's called) has previously included some stunners in colours from dusky pink and cream to black and magenta, and prices from £12 for a wrist strap or £15 for a clutch, right through to £55 or so. My top picks: a simple, retro clutch in soft gold with optional strap (£25) or a pink hard-case with golden, metal laser-cut-style butterflies draped across it (£35).

Cover-ups at Accessorize are mostly in the way of scarves and stoles on the whole – I've seen delicately coloured 100% silk ones start from £12 and go all the way up to £25. There have been elegant patterns to add a touch of detail to simple bridesmaid dresses – a cherry blossom pattern was in the £12 range – and soft, ombre stoles to accompany your own chic shade in colours from black to aqua to pink (£25).

Coast
They've really gone all-out on this wedding malarkey, have Coast – and it's landed us with some interesting bag options in the £25 to £100 range. Colours have been known to go from black to gold via pink and white and back again, but certain standouts have had the moxie to make their mark on me: a nude, modern clutch with detachable silver chain and stretch of lace was £45; a creamy, faux-pearl-encrusted oval was £60; and a modern bride's dream – white covered with a criss-cross of rose-gold-style metal, all with its very own pink metallic snake chain – was £65.

When it comes to keeping us cosy, their springtime offering tends mostly towards wraps in various colours – think a white one edged with pearls for £35 – but I've also seen feather boleros for the statement/vintage-y among us: a deep blue, bow-tied tippet was £55, while the bridal-white versions included a fluffy-as piece for £60, or a more sedate shoulder-hugger for the same spends. In winter, look out for faux fur that's snuggly and – since it's Coast – often even fully lined. Expect to pay roughly between £55 and £150.

Debenhams

There's plenty of choice in clutches and cover-ups at Debenhams – not least of all because they happen to carry a lot of Coast. In their own in-house range, I've seen several pretty bow-decked clutches ranging from £10 to £18, as well as an elegant light-gold twist-front clutch from Star by Julien Macdonald (£25). But the real one to watch here is of course the No. 1 Jenny Packham collection – think satin clutch smothered in clusters of pearls and diamantes (£30) or a luxe purse-style clutch with beading, sequins, diamantes and a silver-bauble clasp (£50).

Cover-ups are similarly classy, with prices ranging from £14.99 to £100 at the time of writing. If you only have time to pop into one shop and pick up your last-minute cosy-upper, make it Debs for the sheer variety: last time I checked a Debut ivory, striped pashmina was £15, a sequin bolero was £28 or a faux-fur cape was £42; a No. 1 Jenny Packham cream, scalloped capelet with pearly detail was £45; a Darling cream bolero with tiered lace was £69; or a Jon Richard off-the-shoulder lace wrap with ribbon tie was £85. And believe me, that was just the tip of the ivory-and-cream iceberg.

Monsoon

With an accessories arm as trendsetting as Accessorize, Monsoon don't need to go out of their way on the bridal-bag front – but they do anyway, because, y'know, they can. In the past their four catch-all pretties were a purse-style clutch encrusted with creamy pearls (£55), a woven pouchette glinting with diamante swirls (£39), a light-blue box clutch with elaborate, vintage-style patterning (£49) and the real glitterbox: a diamante-covered clutch with circular crystal clasp detailing (£85).

When it comes to staying chic and toasty, if it's pure and simple, it's gonna be there. Their capsule collection of wedding cover-ups has been known to nail three ever-popular basics: the cap-sleeved, curve-hemmed ivory shrug (£49), the long-sleeved, wintry equivalent (£69) and the one I kept on my radar for ages – the short-sleeved faux-fur number (£65).

Phase Eight

There's something very grown-up-vintage about Phase Eight: it's like going through a dressing-up box and realising it's all back in fashion. Previously you could dig out the *Downton* days in the shape of a dusky pink clutch patterned all over with tube-shaped beads (£49), go back even further with a cream satin clutch topped off with a big, jaunty bow and bubbly, odd-sized pearls (£49) or update old-school crochet in the form of a white box-clutch with floral appliqué and delicately diamante-flecked clasp (£49).

RE warm-wear: their short-sleeved, textured white bolero would have been short and sweet over a simple white bri-gown (£69), and the snuggle-your-face-into-it long-sleeved angora bolero was the easy-glam winter cosier of my white-wedding dreams for £65 – just add snow.

First-Night Undies

We've all bought pants before – we know where to get his tighty-whities and our strapless, backless, push-up-and-out contraptions. What I'm talking about is a little pre-bow-chicka-wow-wow luxe – first-night style. And contrary to popular belief, that *doesn't* have to mean white...

Ayten Gasson

I love their stuff. I can vouch for the quality. Back when I was a writer at *You & Your Wedding*, their lovely owner sent me a pair of peach silk knickers that are subtly sexy *and* a good fit. For our purposes though, they tend to be a bit on the pricey side, so I'd recommend popping by during sale season – or when you've got your willpower on.

If you *do* shell out, you can at least expect to get that bit more for your money here: their full-price bridal collection has included the 'White Gift Set' with silk garter, jasmine and vanilla scented tea-lights, natural oat soap and handmade knickers finished with a genuine vintage button (£48).

As for sale time: I've seen a gorgeously detailed white organic silk bodysuit reduced from £107 to £39, a peachy-pink lace-trimmed camisole that was £74, now £20 and a lovely lacy, apple-green bralet down from £56 to – count it – £10.

Boux Avenue

If you want it white, Boux Avenue have got plenty to please you right there in their bridal collection. In the past that's meant a delicate lace thong (£8), pretty satin shorts (£12), saucy suspender belt (£16), silk and mesh plunge bra (£28) and semi-see-through, lacefied satin chemise (£35).

If you're thinking something sexier, seek out their babydolls, basques and 'slips' – which aren't what your mother knows them as, but thigh-skimming satin skirts with a cheeky split. They've done everything from a pink, centre-split babydoll with sequinned cups (£40) to a boned corset in dusky pink and black lace (£65), or, if you were really going for it, a scarlet bust-to-hip corset trimmed with sexy-playful ruffles of black mesh (£60). *Rowwwr!*

Freya

You don't shop at Freya for the usual white stuff (though they've got it, up to a K-cup, if you must) – you come here for a two-piece bra and knicker set in oh-so-girlie patterns and colours. I admit it: I've gazed adoringly at their amethyst pairing with blue and yellow butterfly print (bra £32, brief £14), there's been some quiet coveting of a bright and cheerful lime duo with pastel embroidery peeking from the bust (bra £30, short £12) and I nearly gave in to the temptation of a dark green leaf-and-spot-print bralet with red lace trim and matching thong (top £32, bottom £12). Get your getup here and let the fun begin!

Gossard

If you never gave a damn about 3D printing before, you're about to once you browse the Gossard website. Because *damn* do these guys know sexy – and you're going to want what they've got *right now*.

Their full-price bras have been known to start from a teeny-tiny £17, but if you ask me, the hottest mamas are often around the £30 mark. For lovers of traditional white I've spied the Superboost Lace, available in smooth T-shirt cup (that's that £17-er) or lace-all-over plunge (£29) – it's the perfect mix of coy colouring and confidence-rocketing support.

For something seriously sexually charged – but on the right side of tawdry – I'd go for their corselets. Two have topped my lust-have list in the past: the 1940s 'Ooh La La' smothered in intricate lace in shades of pink, grey and black (£59) and the retrolution slip – a gorgeous vintage, blush number with an un-stay-away-able plunging V-neck (£69). Just let him *try* and keep his eyes off you.

Mimi Holliday by Damaris

You don't get much more fun than draping yourself round the doorway wearing a pair of Mimi Holliday's star-covered lace cat ears. Sadly they're £135, so they won't be making our list (ahem, Topshop have been known to do similar cat ears for under £10). The rest of their totally lace-loving range, however, is generally more acceptably priced – though it is, admittedly, at the higher end of our scale. My advice: if £50-odd for a bra is out of your pocket-bracket, shop in the sale or pick their out-of-season stuff up with as much as 65% off at – you guessed it – THEOUTNET.COM.

Long have I daydreamed of me and the black lace, silk and satin Luna Belle shoulder bra heading off into the sale-time sunset – all integrated straps and corset-style ribbon front, let's be honest: it's as irresistible to me as it would be to him (£56). The Bisou Bisou Frost and Blossom collections were more trad-bride-friendly when I was eyeing them up though: think super-sweet white thong with bow back (£37) or a pretty lace and satin suspender belt (£40).

Passionata

I admit it: the same way Benefit make-up draws me in with its witty-pretty packaging, Passionata got me hooked years ago with their fun-off-the-charts retro-cute poster campaign. Spend 10 seconds on their website and you'll see what I mean.

These days they've got points of sale all over the place, but if you need to snap them up online, get their kit off the likes of ASOS or Figleaves. There was a time when I was majorly into their super-sweet-yet-sexy Passio Cherie top with suspenders – the panelled lace, bodice ruching and teeny-striped under-bust bow had me at 'hello', but the price was what really got me on board (£48 for the set at Figleaves). Brides after snow-white selections would feel the same about their delicate White Nights balconette bra (£34) and matching shorty with dainty flower-edge detail (£24).

THEOUTNET.COM

Just another thing to love about THEOUTNET.COM: they make Calvin Klein, Elle Macpherson Intimates, Rigby & Peller and Stella McCartney wearable on your wedding night. The only catch is getting in quick and maxing your chances of finding something in your size.

At the time of writing, their best white bras were a CK lace plunge in a 30D (was £36, now £18) and a Mimi Holliday by Damaris in a 28A, B and C (once £51, now £25.50). Their new-in stuff included a beautiful Elle Macpherson Intimates grey-lace bra that had been available in 32A, 34A, 32B, 32C, 34C, 32D and 34D. My pick of the bunch? A Rigby & Peller black satin bra with lace laid beneath the straps like little cap shoulders – down from £95 to £28.50, at one time it was available in sizes from 30D to 38G.

Victoria's Secret

Think of the iconic US undie-brand and you think of their models – the impossibly sexy Miranda Kerr, for one. But it turns out there's more to the saucy label from the Land of Stars and Stripes than the women who work it on their catwalks.

With boutiques landing all over Britain and stocking everything from satiny white babydolls to cheesy-fun 'I do' tank tops – even 'Bride' hoodies with engagement-ring-style zip pulls (hands up: my Texas-based MOH got me one of these for the wedding morning, and I *love* it!) – we're starting to get the idea over here: Vicky's secret might just be their light-hearted, fun and flirty feel. This could even be lingerie with a *sense of humour*.

And down at brass tacks? I've spied US prices around the $38-mark for a full-price babydoll (plunging to $29.50 in the sale) – that translated to about £23.23 at the time of writing. And even if the UK prices don't follow the exchange rate and just go from dollars to sterling, they're still not out of the realms of possibility for a sexy-fun first night.

Ties and Pocket Squares

If he's not going for the dapper, dishevelled bad-boy look (and come on, what *would* your gran think?) he's going to need the three man-cessories: cufflinks – for which he has a choice of the below and the fine establishments in the Rings and Grooms sections – and ties and pocket squares from these good fellas.

ASDA

If he's a straightforward stripes-or-bust kinda guy, he wants to be getting his groom on at ASDA. The cheapest single, full-price ties are regularly a mere £3 – indecisive types can grab the lot – and then there are the two-packs at about £5 a pop. Hankies – yes, that's totes the same as a pocket square – are usually about £4 or £5 for three patterned or five white, and styles are largely striped, gingham or checked. It's as easy as that.

ASOS

It's not in ASOS's DNA to do things simply. Sure, they've stocked £6 slim black and blue ties, but then there was the bit of their collection that was all grey and white triangles (£8) and bird-print bows (£8). Pocket squares followed suit, though you're not likely to find them to match – I've spied patterns including fish and camouflage-print (£5 each) or a flash of red and black paisley that was seriously Lord-of-the-First-Dance (£12).

BHS

BHS ties usually go from plain colour to stripes and dots, skinny to wide and roughly £5 to £10 – but don't think they're behind the times: among the black and blue I've found red, light grey, purple and even pale pink. Pocket squares-wise I've spied a five-pack of criss-crossed and striped Jack Reids for £6 – and you can't say fairer than that – but you can also expect them to pop up with other groom-essentials in matching sets.

Burton

I'll be honest: I went into Burton expecting the usual stripes and spots malarkey – what I got was a totally wearable breath of fresh air. Obviously they had your salmon skinny ties for £6 and your plain and patterned pocket squares in burgundy, blue and white for £7 – surprisingly the odd dogstooth and even car pattern came in at £7 – but it's what happened at the £7 to £10 marker that really got me thinking: a thick, navy knitted tie (£7), a red geo-patterned 'heritage' number (£8) and a brown tweed skinny (£10). Could good old, dependable Burtons be becoming a trendsetter?

Debenhams

To go with their mammoth collection of shirts, Debenhams rightly always has an epic selection of ties – and they're usually by big dogs from Thomas Nash and Red Herring (about £9.50 to £12.50 full price) to Jasper Conran, Jeff Banks, Osborne (all often around £20) and Piscador (more like £22). With all this bloke-power, tie patterns tend to be just about any manly-elegant thing you could think of, from spots and stripes to flowers and elephants, and I'd certainly say they're worth a look-see if you've got very particular plans in mind.

To go-with good old Debs stocks a helluva lot of white pocket squares – expect to pay from about £6 for three – but in the past I've also seen black-bordered styles (£10) and Osborne's spotted or plain black, red and blue silks (£10). The best value I've spied here for forgetful grooms or truckloads of ushers: 10 Osborne whities for £10.

John Lewis
John Lewis's ties rarely come cheap but hey, these are quality pieces of neckwear. At the time of writing their sale meant prices started from £12.50, but ordinarily you'd be looking at more like £16-plus. It was all very smart and decent – even if there was the odd flash of lemon yellow (£20) – with words like silk, twill and Eton thrown around all over the place after about £19.50. Pocket squares came in trippy colours but for the most part were silly money (upwards of £29 each).

Marks & Spencer
Marks & Sparks ties have been known to start from a very respectable £5, and go right up to the Savile Row Inspired selection for £29.50. They've done plains, stripes, dots and even bubbles down in single digits, rising to flowers, paisley and check with the bumping-up of numbers. Last time I checked your classic pure-silk wedding cravat came in 11 colours and was joined by a matching pocket square for £12.50 – but if you'd rather pick your own nose-dabbers, they started from £5 for five whites and went through grey, purple and blue checks and stripes.

Next
This being Next, they know their way around both trad and contemporary ties – as well as a jolly good mishmash of both. They've started from £8 and gone up to £65 for some sneaky Thomas Pinks, but at the time of writing your best bets were the plain-coloured tie and hanky sets (£10) or, if you were

going super-smart, the bow-tie, cummerbund and cufflinks set (£18). There was also a good selection of pocket squares in gold, burgundy, silver and plum (£8 each), while patterned paisley and dots were £4 a pop.

River Island

I half-expected the cool kids at River Island to have eschewed the whole concept of a tie and created some freaky twisted shapes to wrap around our collars. Not so: last time I looked they'd done the hipper thing and rolled out both geo-print and grey denim bow-ties (£8 each), a grey metallic skinny tie (£10) and a charcoal textured tie (£10), all of which could be pinned with either a gold-tone hexagonal or spiky gunmetal collar pin (£6). Pocket squares were a similarly insanely modish affair – think blue paisley-printed silk (£8) and navy tribal print (£6).

Tesco

For the most part, think stripes, checks, dots and flowers when you think ties at F&F – and expect to pay about £3 to £5 a pair, or £8 to £10-ish with matching shirt. Pocket squares tend towards the plain or dotty division, but often come in standard shades like white, black, blue and burgundy for about £3 each.

Tie Rack

Ties are, kind of, their *thing* at Tie Rack, and don't you know it: from plain to paisley, Union Jack to flowers and black to bright red, I've always been impressed by their confident, metro style (mostly £14.99 to £29.99). They also know their cravats – I've seen them for £22.99 in black, navy or red or reduced from £19.99 to £6.87 in gold. Meanwhile, the finishing touch – the pearl-ended cravat pin – was just £9.99. There was the odd striped or chain-linked pocket square, but mostly they went for quality over fuss: plain shades of fine Italian silk for about £9.99 a go.

Topman

I've said it before and I'll say it again: Topman are *mental*. But in that cult, so-bonkers-it-looks-like-fun kind of a way. At the time of writing, as well as off-white (£6) and geo-patterned (from £6 to £3) pocket squares, they had possibly the skinniest ties I've ever seen for £8 (can anyone beat 3cm?), ombre flannel ties in various shades (£10), three black ties covered in studs (£10) and my personal fave: a thin, mostly rectangular, brown leather bow-tie (£8). Come on, cut loose!

CHAPTER 8

Hair & Beauty

Putting your face on needn't cost an arm and a leg

I'm a sensible, adult human. I know it shouldn't be this important. But when my hair looks bad I feel like Oscar the Grouch, just crawled out of my trash can. And this is from someone who never feels like she has the time to blow-dry – if you actually take care of your hair, it must be even more important it looks good on your big day.

Make-up? Hands up: I'm bad at it at the best of times – I didn't master the art of liner until the age of 25, and that still doesn't include the liquid stuff. If you're anything like me, you're going to need help to pull off the whole 'blushing bride' thing – but who says it has to be from a professional?

Before You Start
If you *are* capable of doing your own hair and make-up, if you're one of those girls who spends twenty-five minutes every morning and walks out the door looking like perfection, then don't believe the hype: you don't have to let a pro do it if you've got the skills

for the face and the 'do you want. *Especially* the face. Because you do want to marry your H2B looking like you, the girl he fell in love with, right?

If you're the kind of ham-fisted incompetent that I am though (and believe me, *no-one* is as bad at this stuff as me) you're going to need to draft someone else in. Who that is will vary – just give some of my suggestions a chance and if they don't come off, head to the pros with my blessing (and my tips for spending less).

Issue a Draft

Your sister, your best friend, your auntie – we all know at least one flawless girl. Someone who's so put-together you imagine she must have got up at the crack of dawn. But if she did, wouldn't there be bags under her eyes? Are they hiding under a layer of foundation? Does she even *wear* foundation?

For me, that's my little sis'. She's been showing me up since she hit puberty with her mastery of alien tools like the blusher brush and hairdryer. She even went and became a hairdresser and learned about things like *dye* and *extensions*. So naturally when it came to my big day, it was her standing behind my chair with a million hairgrips.

Whoever your closet-pro is, draft them in for your big day. Make it their wedding present to you and save time, stress and – you guessed it – moolah. With their expertise comes a girlie evening of hair and make-up trials, and someone there on the day for occasional touch-ups without charging you by the hour.

The only things to watch out for? One: just because they know and love you doesn't mean they're at your beck and call. Be sensitive to busy times in their lives and the fact that they want to have fun on your day too – they're *not* your personal beauty slave.

Two: pick someone with whom you can be totally open and honest – and someone who listens to you. If you know you can't tell your poor, sweet auntie that you absolutely *hate* that wonky top-knot and facial glitter, don't ask her. If you know she wouldn't listen if you did say something, close your eyes, imagine your wedding photos, and go somewhere else.

Best for: Brides with truly talented friends and relatives – preferably who are on your wavelength with regard to what's hot and what's, just, *not*.

YouTube Sensei

You can learn anything on YouTube. But that doesn't mean you *should*. Trying to balance a second mirror behind you on your wedding day so you can see your hands pushing grips into the back of your head? *Not* the most serene way to start your day. But the same doesn't have to go for your make-up. Unless you were planning on drawing a henna tattoo on the back of your neck there's a good chance you could learn to put on your own face.

If neither of these sounds like something your particular hands will ever be able to do (I still can't curl my own hair, no matter how many videos I watch), draft in a bridesmaid who can learn to do it for you. Show her pictures first – there's no point in her spending a week learning something you might not even want – and don't apply the pressure. Ask her way in advance so you can still go to a pro if needs be.

The best teachers? There are pros from Benefit Cosmetics, MAC Cosmetics, Illamasqua, L'Oréal Paris (destinationbeauty), Topshop, *GLAMOUR* magazine and more on YouTube. So no excuses.

Best for: Brides or maids with pro-potential. This could be the start of a beautiful online friendship…

Live & Loaded (with The Knowledge)

You know those women in Debenhams and House of Fraser who always try to stop you for make-up trials? Try to resist the natural urge to avoid them. Take a seat at, say, the Benefit or Clinique counter, show or tell them what you want, and let them take you through the steps of how to get it.

If you know you're going to feel guilty about not going home with some make-up afterwards, go to a counter you know you can afford and buy only what you really need – if they add a shade to your lips that's spot-on and you don't already have it, for example. Same old black mascara that you can't tell from the one in your handbag? Not so much.

There's another option here: bring your maids along. Get them to watch and give whoever seems to get the idea a promotion to make-up artist on your big day – just remember, she's going to need a mention in at least one speech. While you're there, make sure everyone gets their turn in the chair of they want it – no-one likes a solo pamperer.

Best for: Brides in need of real-life tutoring – when demanding 'how the hell did you just *do* that?!' needs to be a two-way conversation...

Going Pro

If neither you nor your entourage have the skills or the time to suss out the finer points of putting your hair in a chignon, or how to do those damn cat-eye flicks with liquid liner (not that I'm bitter), then your local pro is the way to go (woohoo!). But there's no reason she should cost you as much as your outfit...

Local Love

I say local because the first thing to bear in mind is that, like any supplier, if you pull your hair and make-up artist in from far-off lands, you're likely to end up footing the bill for her travel. This is the first additional cost that needs to be agreed before you book anything.

Even travelling to your house or venue *can* cost extra, however local your laydee – not always, so check with your particular artist.

If she does want to pump up the price and your wedding isn't until the afternoon, consider whether it's feasible to nip into the salon with your maids before the ceremony.

Put Up for Touch-Ups
If your artist does come to you, is she popping in, working her magic, then disappearing for the rest of the day, or were you envisioning her sticking around to tweak your look for the photos?

Bear in mind most will charge per hour for hanging around at your venue, so it might be worth keeping make-up remover and basics for touch-ups in yours or your MOH's clutch instead.

Package Deal
There's a reason I've called her your 'hair and make-up artist': it's almost certainly going to be cheaper to hire one beauty wizard to do both. She won't be charging you double for travel costs for starters, and you'll only have one supplier totting up costs by the hour if you ask her to stay. If you're going into the salon on the day, consider one that has a spa or beauty menu as well as hair options and save time and money with a package that covers both.

Bridal Party
You're bringing this one woman or salon a lot of business – and like anything, you should get it for less if you buy in bulk. Negotiate on price: see whether you can get the total down or, say, reduce the cost of your two maids when you pay full-price for you and your mum.

Maids with Love
Speaking of your maids, remember how they're your best friends? How they love you and they want you to have the best day ever? Think about asking them how they'd feel about doing their own hair and make-up, or perhaps chipping in or even paying for their own. Like discussing who puts up the dollar for their dresses

though, this is something that should be no-pressure, and should be put out there one-to-one.

C'me 'ere, Junior

As with a haircut, getting the salon director to do your 'do is likely to cost more than going with a junior. If you *have* to have her Ladyship, are your maids happy to take a rung down, or to pay the difference if not? Do your mum or friends know stylists who might not own the salon but always do an I-feel-gorgeous job?

The Trials of Trials

You're going to want a practice run at letting someone else get hold of your hair and lippy before the big day. Check how many trials are included in the cost, as you could find they turn out to be an extra. This is especially important if you're going for less-qualified members of staff, or with an artist you've never used before.

Best for: Time-poor or stress-heavy brides who want to hand off thinking about the way they look to someone else. Also complicated make-up and up-dos.

Make-Up

If you're DIY-ing your look, we all know where to pick up affordable make-up – Boots, Superdrug, Debenhams, supermarkets – and it's easy to spot the cheaper brands, too. But in this instance it might actually be worth – *gasp* – investing in a few basics that you know will see you through the whole day.

I'm not saying you should shell out £40 on mascara – just that if you haven't already got your fave brands down pat, bear in mind that this is one day when you're going to be in the spotlight for 24 hours straight. And your make-up needs to be able to go the distance.

This isn't the time to layer on a brand you've never used before at the last minute, only to find it wipes off all over your dress or worse, irritates your skin. If you are going to go for brands you're not familiar with, make sure that you've tried and tested them for staying power and sensitivity.

Also, bear in mind it might be worth going for the everlasting lippy your best friend recommended or the mascara your mum has been faithful to for years, rather than flunking six different cheaper ones and ending up buying the mid-rangers anyway.

Veils

You might not know it yet, but at some point you're going to want to try on a veil. Just try it. See how it feels. For a laugh. Until you want it. When that day comes, resist the urge to splurge £300 on silk edging dripping with diamonds.

You can go for a shorter, simpler style to keep your options wide open, but even if you *have* to have it elaborate, do it the doable way (erm, see below) and get all dressed up without waving bye-bye to those tasty canapés.

Debenhams

On the ribbon-trim rampage? Sit back and relax: the D-store has you covered. I've seen sheer mesh and satin here for 60 smackers (sterling), all thanks to Pearce II Fionda. They've also had some dramatic floor-length Rainbow Club veils, but they're often more around the £99 mark. Stick to shorter styles if you want to pay less – in the past you could get Jon Richard's ivory Italian tulle shoulder-skimmer for £55, or a secondary satin-edge option: his hip-length number in the same fabric for £85.

Lily Bella

There's something oh-so French and feminine about a birdcage veil – the structured style that covers your eyes and nose with net. And if anyone knows a thing or two about them, it would have to be Lily Bella Bird Cage Veil Couture. Before you're scared off by the 'couture' word, check out the prices last time I looked: net veils from £16 or tulle styles from £20. Numbers went up with details like flowers (£25) and feathers (£50), but many started from under £80 or less. Side note: she also happens to do a beautiful collection of bridal belts for about £40 to £60 – perfect if your dress needs some pow!

Monsoon

They weren't exactly rolling in veils when last I checked, but the one they were hawking was an elegant two-tier, silver-beaded scalloped trim that flowed from head to waist, waist to hips (£69). Well, if ever you need a subtle something to justify those silvery heels…

Phase Eight

These are my pick for the bride who likes her veil long and look-at-this: at the sale-time of writing, Phase Eight's aisle-sweeper was £34.50, down from a still-very-reasonable £69. They were also doing a fine-net polyester number that fell to hip length for £29.50 instead of £59.

More, More, More: Many of the affordable brands back in The Dress do their very own lines in accessories. Snoop around their websites or ask at your local bridal boutique for your best bets.

Tiaras & Hair Accessories

You wouldn't believe what you'll pay for some spangly hair clips. Wait for it: £100-plus. I know! Admittedly they're often one-of-a-kind or ever-so-delicately hand-strung, but if you can cope without the VIP treatment, you can often find looks just as lovely for downwards of a tenner. *Whew*.

Accessorize

In case you haven't noticed by now, Accessorize know their way around a hair slide. And a grip. And a comb. In the past you could find faux flowers with pearly detailing (£10), slides with stones in three different colours (six for £7), even hairpins with little oval jewels on the end (four for £10) – and that's just their official occasion collection. Beyond that, there were beaded Alice bands (£7), rose hairpins with crystal centres (four for £7) and elaborately beaded Grecian bandos (£17). All lust-worthy, all purse-friendly, as always.

Debenhams

Prepare to get your princess on big-time at Debs, where at the time of writing I counted no less than 26 different adults' tiaras, ranging in price from £28 to £85. And you've got to hand it to them: most of their collection was by Jon Richard, a name-to-know in Wedding World whose site is worth a double-take of its own.

As always when it comes to head-sparkles, less is less, and the subtle glint at the affordable end of Debs's spectrum featured a few slender twists of diamantes and a couple of flowers of faux pearls (£28). Elsewhere there were rows of crystal filigree flowers by dress designer Alan Hannah (£35), leafy pearl and crystal prettiness again by Jon Richard (£35) and, as we got into the fairly steep range, high, layered look-at-me twists of crystal that would make her Madge proud (Jon Richard, £50). Be ready to take a bow.

Glitzy Secrets

Make no mistake: tiaras at Glitzy Secrets aren't a covert glimmer slipped on to appease your mum – they're beautiful beasties of crystal and faux pearl designed to suit only the simplest dresses or most daring brides.

Last time I looked their collection included side and head-on tiaras at prices from £48 to £126 – expect flowers, butterflies, feathery shapes, twists of Forties glamour and bows. My personal favourite was a side tiara plastered with teeny-weeny crystals to make up one giant, head-turning rose (£64.50).

Combs, clips, pins and slides, on the other hand, offered more understated options – often with a Deco or heirloom twist – and tended towards more like £12 to £68. There were headpieces and hair claws for non-princessy glamour too – think Forties ribbon-style looks (£30) and vintage crystals (£19). Wear Glitzy's secret stash if you want to wow.

CHAPTER 9

The Rings

Just because it's preciousss doesn't mean you should be out of pocket

Ah, the *precioussses*. (Sorry, I couldn't resist.) But seriously, the rings are the only part of your wedding that will be with you every day of your marriage – except, y'know, each other. And since I'd like my ring to last a little longer than the next time I wash up/bake a cake/do anything at all handsy I'm allowing a little more of our budget for these. None of them will go over £500 each but I know that's a bit steep, so I'm also laying out some options for £100 and under.

Before You Start
Oooh, shiny… It's easy to get mesmerised by a beautiful bit of bling or sucked in by teeny-tiny prices. But before you go there, remember there are – as always – a few trusty rules to help make sure you put the *right* ring on it.

Material
Everybody knows platinum is the leader of the pack when it comes

to cost, and a lot of that is because of its rarity, durability and the fact that everybody you know wants a piece. Next in line is the new kid on the block: palladium. They don't broadcast it, but the lesser-known metal is also part of the platinum family. It's not quite so rare, and only about as heavy as silver, but otherwise it's got very similar properties.

Classic gold – in white, rose and yellow – comes next, and of course the colours are special, but it's more than just a pretty face: it might not be as rare, heavy or durable as the platinum family, but it is still weighty and it resists tarnishing much better than silver. Remember that less can be more, too: purer gold – about 22 ct to 24 ct – might have more of the good stuff in it, but it's also softer and less durable than its alloyed allies.

Then there's silver at the super-savings end of the spectrum. Yes, you can easily bag a sterling sparkler for under £100, but remember that silver tarnishes, and depending on the alloy it's plated with it can cause irritation to sensitive skin (nickel tends to be the itch-inducing no-no).

In a nutshell: the higher up the precious-metal food chain you go, the rarer, more durable and more likely to be hypoallergenic you can expect your rings to be.

The same can't be said for the not-so-precious metals. Okay, at the end of the day titanium and stainless steel are nowhere near in short supply, so they're less elite and ladida than their oh-so-desirable cousins, but when it comes to strength, durability and cost, they've got you covered.

Stainless steel is a bit of a misnomer – it's resistant but not completely immune to staining or dulling, but it's easy enough to look after since you don't need special cleaning agents to brighten it up again. It's also pretty damn durable – just be sure to check whether your ring contains that pesky nickel if your skin is sensitive.

Titanium is the one to go for if you're not so into high-shine, since it's naturally more of a matte metal. Don't be fooled by its unbearable lightness of being, though – they use it for stuff like planes and space shuttles because it's just *that* strong. It won't tarnish or rust either, and you sensitive types have no worries – it's totally hypoallergenic. The only thing to watch out for is that you get the sizing right first time, because it can't be altered. Much like your love. (I'll let you choose between 'Awww!' and 'Bleh!')

Weight/Thickness
Obviously, the more, the moneyer. And yes, I just made up that word to fit my own dastardly purposes – mwahahaha! But you get the point: thicker, heavier rings will generally cost you more. Well, that was short and sweet!

Simplicity
Is it just me, or are we starting to notice a pattern here? Oh that's right: simpler = cheaper. It worked for your wedding dress, it will work for your cake and it works for your ring, too. So remember: stones, patterns and engraving will generally push the price north.

Diamonds
If you are going to go for diamonds, be careful where you get them – and keep an eye on the five Cs:

Carats translate to the weight and therefore size of the diamond – would you rather have a perfect little chip off the old block or a less light-catching whopper?

Colour is graded by letters: D, E and F diamonds are totally colour-free so they let more light in (better for your sparkle), but you'd have to get an expert to tell the difference between them and the nearly-colourless G, H and I. There's the tiniest hint of yellow in K, L and M; it's a little more there but still very light in N, O, P, Q and R; and there's even more but it's still light in S through Z.

Clarity is about the itty-bitty blemishes on almost every diamond ever – and this is where your too-good-to-be-true diamonds come in. Shopping channels will show you an absolute rock at an absolutely rock-bottom price, but it's probably the worst clarity other than uncertified: I3.

I3, I2 and I1 diamonds have blemishes *you can see* without putting them under a magnifying glass. Most of the higher clarities: not so much. They improve from the three Is in the following order: SI 2, SI 1, VS2, VS1, VVS2, VVS1, and the nearly-nonexistent IF (internally flawless) and F (flawless).

Cut isn't the same as shape – it's not about ending up with a heart or a round diamond, it's about getting the proportions right so you get the maximum twinkle-factor. In order of best to worst, most jewellers call the cuts: ideal, premium, very good, good, fair and poor. Most of these are pretty sparkly besides the fair and poor cuts – with those you're likely to get a hefty hunk of diamond that barely glitters.

Conflict-free. This one's up to you, but I'd rather ask for proof that the diamond I'll be wearing for the rest of my life didn't cost someone else's.

Then there's the setting. Talk to your jeweller about this one, but make sure your diamond is set in a metal that's sturdy enough not to wear away and let your stone loose. It's also worth considering the height of your setting if you want to wear it every day – who wants to catch their diamond on clothes, tea towels and the rest all day long?

Let's go Bling-Hunting

Remember, you don't have to buy a *wedding band*, you can just buy a *ring*. As long as it's made of sturdy, hardwearing material, it doesn't have to come off the – likely marked-up – *wedding rings* tray.

Family Heirlooms

I'm not suggesting you prise Nana's wedding ring off her finger while she's sleeping, but maybe your kindly old Grammy – or even your mum or dad – has a perfect ring going spare that they hadn't thought to hand down to you.

If you've got the kind of open, relaxed relationship with your olds that doesn't necessitate rifling through their belongings while they're out, why not ask if there's anything they'd like to give as your wedding present? You'll probably find there's a lovely little story behind your inherited gem that you can keep alive when you hand it down to your granddaughter.

Best for: Barely-there-budget brides and grooms and ones with closely held family values. Also ones who want to be part of a history that started before they did.

Old-School Steals

A wise man once told me that he liked to buy second-hand things because it was fun to imagine where they'd been and what they'd seen. It's not about fishing other people's throwaways out of the proverbial dustbin – it's about giving new life and new stories to a beautiful, forgotten thing. If this sounds like you, the pre-owned route could be the perfect way to find your wedding rings.

Hidden Gems

Gotcha! Bet you didn't think I was going to harp on about local business again, did you? That's why I craftily titled this one something secretive and lured you in. But seriously: I don't know all the little second-hand, pawn, charity or antique shops and auction rooms near you that might have your dream band stashed away. Go forth and discover.

Bentley & Skinner

It's not like it looks on *Bargain Hunt* and co. – rooting through jumble sales in the hope of stumbling across a stonker. Get a feel for the kind of glam jewels you could be browsing in the comfort of Bentley & Skinner's website. At the time of writing, there was a rose gold Victorian solitaire going for £395 in their Antique & Period Collection, as well as several 18-carat yellow gold bands for under £450 in their Modern Jewellery section – with and without the beautiful, delicately milled edge.

Best for: Vintage-lovers, story-seekers and couples looking for the kind of quality that's usually out of their price range.

Tailor-Made
If your idea of making your rings your own means more than an engraving, or you're head-over-heels for a style you can't afford in the shop, having something similar tailor-made by the right jeweller can cut the cost.

The Man with a Plan
Haha! Did it again! How many times are you going to fall for this? Oh, you wanted to talk local outfits. Well, um, alright then. You'll often find clever little craftsmen squirrelled away in your city centre who know a thing or two about bashing out something beautiful by their own fair hand – and since they've got the high street to compete with, a lot of them will do them at *less than high-street prices*, so they're definitely worth a chat.

Seventy Seven Diamonds
So many options, so little time required. Click over to 77's site and bish, bash, bosh – you could have your dream plain or stone-set band designed, sized and shopped in a matter of minutes. Last time I had a little play, a size J, white gold, 1.7mm thick, 2mm-width ring set with *three* G-colour, VS-clarity diamonds came to £390.28. I also experimented with a size S, platinum, 2.1mm thick, 2.5mm-width traditional plain band, which came out at £346.10. Punch in your deets and see.

Best for: Low-budget and just-so brides who can see their dream ring now – just not outside their imaginations.

Band Brands

Wedding rings, get your wedding rings here! Whether you're in the market for a classic band, a subtle sparkler, a rocky mountain or a totally unexpected stunner, here are the brands for swish styles to suit budgets great and small.

Alex Monroe

Nature – that's from flowers and birds to animals and insects – is the buzzword (geddit?) at Alex Monroe. The kind of delicate, pretty creations you can't help but handle with awe, reverance and care, they're spot-on if you're a walker, horsey type or animal lover who's after something alternative and symbolic.

At the time of writing, prices started at £120 for 22ct gold plate or £96 for sterling silver. The most expensive ring in our price range was 18ct solid gold for £475, but this isn't the place for affordable white gold or platinum – or for him.

Argos

You don't get much more straightforward than Argos – I've seen them sell a super-skinny 9ct gold, rolled-edged, unisex wedding band for £24.99, so there you go. At the time if you upgraded to 18ct gold you could get rings with more width and still spend under £100. Alternatively, palladium ranged from £79.99 to £329.99 – a diamond-inset design (no details available) was £259.99. Even the elusive platinum was all within our budget if you went for a simple band: it ranged from £299.99 to £479.99 – and that goes for his ring too.

Astley Clarke

There are always some shiners with a difference over at Astley Clarke – though most of them aren't under 'wedding rings'. In the nuptial category last time I checked I found only two styles sitting pretty within our budget: an elegant Monica Vinader eternity ring in sterling silver (£275) or an 18ct white gold 'sparkle ring' – 4mm width with a fairly spectacular minutely hammered finish (£290).

Out there in the rest of the rings was everything from slim sterling silver for £45 to ultra-thin 18ct gold with a solitaire diamond for £295. Then there was Carolina Bucci's quirky woven ring in 18ct yellow gold and cream silk (£245).

Not sure why there's a video of a woman wrapping your ring up on the website, but hey ho, at least you know it'll look good for the postman. This one's an offbeat stop for classy or unusual pieces in decent metals – but be prepared to pass up their more expensive platinum and diamond glitterballs.

Beaverbrooks

Platinum can be pretty pricey at Beaverbrooks except around sale time – and even then I last spotted only one design in our price range: a band set with eight 0.05 carat, H colour, SI1 clarity diamonds (£476). Twit-twoo!

Meanwhile, a 9ct white gold and cubic zirconia number was reduced from £175 to £108, whereas their cheapest 18ct plain gold band would set you back £200 (down from £450). They're not our cheapest entry by any means, and you're unlikely to get anything all that unusual here, but they're good for a timeless style in a quality, solid metal.

CRED Jewellery

If you like your glittery things with a conscience, try CRED's Fairtrade and Fairmined rings set with ethical jewels. Expect styles that are simple, most roughly in the £290 to £485 bracket and available in 18ct yellow or white gold – some I've seen set with little stones or engraved with lines or scrolls. There have also been a handful of interesting extras over in 'detailed wedding rings' – think gold-plated branches with or without diamonds between about £60 and £100.

If it was me, I'd forget about their platinum – it tends to be out of our price range – and only go bespoke if you can afford the £120 non-refundable deposit.

Ernest Jones
I like Ernest Jones. I'm biased. My Leo Diamond engagement ring is from there, and it comes with a little code you can put in online to see the journey your diamond made. It also comes in about three boxes just in case it didn't feel special enough that the man I love wanted me to wake up next to him forever.

But that's not a reason for you to love them – this is: there are classically elegant rings aplenty in our price range. When last I looked, the cheapest men's band under 'wedding rings' was a rather suave brushed-titanium number for £75, while for women it was a 9ct yellow gold court ring for £119. Upgrades to 18ct gold started around the £250 mark, while palladium got a look-in from £150. For platinum you were looking at at least £325 here, which went up that bit more according to width and/or weight.

F. Hinds
Style at F. Hinds pretty much walks the line, but with that swinging step you did off curbs when you were a kid – simple gold bands are twisted for a little kink, palladium is brushed for a matte finish, or white gold is engraved with stars or prettily swirled or beaded.

If you're after a timeless style with a so-you difference, this is the place to go – not least because a lot of it's in our price range. My most recent investigation brought up a simple, 3mm palladium ring as their cheapest for women, at £89.95. For men it was the 5mm equivalent for £159. Gold started at £135 for 9 carats or £240 for 18, or you were looking at £399-plus for platinum.

Georg Jensen
If you've got your heart set on anything more resilient than sterling silver, don't go to Georg. It's not that they don't do it – there's plenty of gorgeous gold – but at the time of writing, prices on

anything other than a simple 18ct gold ring (£465 for white, £495 for yellow) were on another planet.

If silver suits, though, Jensen's is the jewellery equivalent of a sweet shop: there are just so many sleek, unusual styles. I've drooled over everything from looping twists at £160 to raised orbs of amethyst for £190, or thick, wavy chunks inspired by things like geometry and Scandinavian rivers from £165 to £200. Let loose in the crazy-chic boutique – just be prepared to do plenty of essential silver-polishing.

Goldsmiths

Goldsmiths are another one for classic styles with a modern finish – think men's titanium, striped matte and shiny, with a 0.05-carat diamond inset, or a ladies' twisted Celtic-style ring that looks like gold-dipped twigs. In the past prices have started at £59 for a men's titanium band, while 9ct gold began at £119, 18ct gold at £379, palladium at £329 (6mm) and platinum at £479 (2mm). My standout? A 7mm gents' palladium ring with a thick, brushed strip and polished edges (£429). Swoon!

H. Samuel

Samuel's is the place for classic wedding polish. That's not to say there isn't the odd contemporary number, but most of what you see will be pretty and timeless. That means simple metal, twists of diamonds or patterned etching, plus occasional bi- or tri-colour gold combos. Last time I checked them out, a sale on a men's titanium band meant their cheapest wedding ring was a brushed style with indented stripe for £29.99 (reduced from £59.99). Gold started at £89.99 for 9 carats, £199 for 18 carats or £199 for two tones, while palladium was upwards of £249 and platinum £399-plus.

Laura Lee

Delicate and vintage are the watchwords at Laura Lee, so old-school romantics can expect to fall head over heels. Styles are super-slim and unpredictable: they range from the likes of wiry 9ct yellow-gold bands topped with tiny rubies, sapphires or diamonds (from £175) to 18 carats of rose-gold plating finished with a blue cameo of a whippet (£225). Almost all are usually in our price range and many even offer the chance for you to tweak metals and gemstones until they're practically perfect. As a wordsmith and a French fan, I only have eyes for the 18ct rose-gold plated band engraved with 'Rien Que Toi, Moi, Nous' – 'Nothing but you, me, us'.

Links of London
It's a brand name that strikes fear into my heart – mostly because I know I'm going to struggle to resist it. But there's no need: I've seen sterling silver from £85, simple bands of 18ct gold at £350 for 2mm or £450 for 3mm, and 18ct gold bubbles entwined around tiny white or 'black' (read: bluish) pearls for £350. Stop by in the sales and get more bling for your buck: I've watched an 18ct rose-gold ring shaped like a heart go for £420 instead of £600. But whenever you decide to rock up, expect original, contemporary, boundary-pushing styles galore.

Mappin & Webb
Keeping it sleek and simple for your W-day? Then you might find some options among Mappin & Webb's clean, bright wedding bands. Don't be lured by the promise of rows of rubies and orange sapphires – at the time of writing, none of their stone-set rings were in our price range. Instead, come for gold that started at a minimum of 18 carats from £295, and flashes of palladium from £175. Platinum was less promising at this particular pitstop, where it was upwards of £495.

Monica Vinader
Stones, beautiful stones – white topaz and citrine… Most of Monica Vinader's bling-tastic rings are no shrinking violets – expect epic cuts of semi-precious gems wrapped in lacework or simply strewn

metals. Many styles let you choose between sterling silver or 18ct yellow- or rose-gold-plated vermeil. You can switch stones, too – often from labradorite to moonstone or amethyst to aqua chalcedony. Previously, prices ranged from about £35 to £240 – but that's before you started whacking on those size, metal or stone selections.

Pandora
They don't just do charm bracelets. Who knew? What they do do is a collection of ever-so-girlie, seriously pretty, mostly silver rings. Even in the gold section. It's rarely white gold with yellow gold, so be careful – it's mostly silver with just a touch of the yellow stuff. That's fine if sterling's what you want, but if you'd rather go for something more hardwearing, your choice is oh-so-elegant but more limited. Rather than the webs of flowers (£150) or solo roses (£95) you could get in silver, expect the likes of delicate pods of pave diamonds in 18ct yellow gold (£335), loops of 3D hearts in 14ct yellow gold (£315), or similar pods of 0.07ct diamonds in 18ct white gold (£440).

Tesco
Don't expect any of that fancy-schmancy palladium or platinum stuff at Tesco, but last time I looked they'd do you a sterling silver band from £18 or a 9ct gold one from £30. If all you're after is something simple – glossy or matte gold, maybe with a few incy-wincy diamonds or a satin-finished stripe – most rings here were under £130 and they'd do the job. Just bear in mind that you're unlikely to find much above 9ct.

Tiffany & Co.
I know your wallet just went into spasm, but give it a little stroke – you can afford more than you think at Tiffany if you know where to look. On their site, don't be fooled by the rings landing page, which hints that they only do silver, gold and white gold – there's rose gold, platinum, titanium and more tucked away.

Your best bet to see all the styles you can afford is to go into All Rings, then search according to price range. I've found sterling silver, titanium and stainless steel under £200, in designs like a beaded band engraved with 'I love you' (£160), three rows of open hearts (£185) or Paloma Picasso's handwriting-esque 'XOXO' pattern (£135).

Further up the cost chain, there was plenty to pick from that was still under £500, including 2mm of milgrain-edged 18ct rose gold (£445), an Elsa Peretti, Diamonds by the Yard thin twist of 18ct yellow gold linked to a 0.07ct round diamond (£445), or a masculine, car-inspired stainless steel and titanium beast partly engraved with a criss-cross pattern (£365). Just be careful of the sizings before you give them your heart (and your debit card) – they can sometimes be teeny-weeny.

Best for: Fuss-free ring shopping in a range of classic or contemporary styles – and in materials to suit any bank balance. Also a good bet for whirlwind weddings that can't wait for the post or fit in vintage-trawling.

Online

Squinting at your laptop monitor might not be the most romantic way to shop for wedding rings, but it can turn up some like-nothing-else styles at surprising prices. The trick is not to assume it must be cheapest 'cause it's on the world wide window-shop – re-read the opening of this section and make sure you're getting something special for your spends.

While you're there, don't forget to check your seller's reviews – maybe even touch base by email – and know your refund rights before you order anything.

Amazon

Ah, Amazon. Known for books and DVDs, it's also the humble home to a shocking amount of wedding bands: at last count, 400 pages. You can go right in and search for 'wedding rings', or you can schlep over to their ring store, where at the time of writing the top two listings were a £2,731 set of diamond wedding and engagement blinders, and a stainless-steel-masquerading-as-yellow-gold Elvish-inscribed number from *Lord of the Rings* (down from £31.99 to £7.99, since you're asking).

If I were you, I'd head to the Ring Store, click into Wedding Rings, click your preferred deets down the left-hand side (e.g. white gold) and type £0 to £500 (or your own magic number) into the Price section. That way you'll quickly whittle down the scrolling and spy your stunner – like the 3mm platinum ring that was reduced from £527.64 to £209.59 back when I was looking.

eBay

If you've got the time – and the reflexes – for a quick-fire round of bids, the original online auction site is worth dipping into. Just be sure to do your research on the ring you want – and keep an eye out for extra charges like P&P, so you don't spend over the odds.

Etsy

Antique Engagement, Designer Vintage and Titanium Wedding Bands were all sections of the Etsy Fine Jewellery landing page when I stopped by. Shop Art Deco, Edwardian, Victorian and other eras, as well as brand new rings by independent designers. If you're after something with the wow-where-did-you-*get*-that!? factor, this place has some serious potential.

MyFlashTrash

If you're not after a style that's utterly off its rocker, look away now. The blimmin' batty brand pumps out everything from 18ct rose-gold plated rings set with gothic black skulls eating citrine stones (£255) to grinning monsters made of 9ct-gold-plated silver with glittering garnet eyes (£415). Rock and/or *roll*.

Notonthehighstreet.com

Handmade, organic, ethical or personalised mean anything to you? Then the indie sellers at notonthehighstreet.com could be your guys. I've come across a rustic organic gold ring from SH & LH for £370, an ethical, 18ct palladium and white gold band from Lilia Nash Jewellery for £238, and a sterling silver bespoke fingerprint ring from Patrick Laing for £285. Lush.

Very

They've got the simple bands and the classic etching, as well as the odd smattering of diamonds or hunk of gorgeous semi-precious stone over at Very. The affordable end of the scale has been known to rock the likes of a chunky titanium ring with brushed middle and shiny edging (£25), as well as a silver, 4mm ladies' band (£35). Gold has started around the £94 mark with 3mm of shiny 9ct yellow or white, then broken the 18ct barrier around £235. At the same time, palladium showed its face at £355 in the shape of a 5mm court, but platinum pipped it to the post with a slimline band for £280. *Very* good show, wot?

Best for: Out-of-hours wedmin. Log on anytime of day or night and get the goods sorted at your convenience.

CHAPTER 10

The Cake

Luscious layers that won't pile on the pounds

If you bake it, they will come... But they'll probably still turn up if you get it from Marks's. Because there's more than one way to ice a cake – whether your granny mixed the batter with her own fair hand or you whipped it out of a box the day before.

Before You Start
Yes, I'm sneaking it in here now. If you want the professional touch, shop around at your local bakers before writing them off. Prices will vary, and even if you can't afford your classic three-tier, white behemoth, they might be able to offer you too-gorgeous-to-eat options like cupcakes or the other pretties I get into below. If you *can* afford the real deal – or you *have* to find a way to – here are a few cost-cutting suggestions that work, whichever way you slice it.

Design
This is the big kahuna. Because you've probably seen at least one rerun of *Choccywoccydoodah* (well, it *is* essential wedding research)

and now have your heart set on a three-foot sugar-craft mound of love hearts draped in jewels.

Or not. But seriously, if you've got anything too complicated on your mind, it's going to take extra bakerpower that you'll end up paying for. Instead, try to downsize your original idea without losing the core of it – if you were dreaming of five tiers enrobed in icing that's designed to look like the lace of your dress, make it three tiers of straight white icing, but wrap a real piece of lace around each.

Oh, and think about the *type* of icing too – even consider a sprinkling of icing-sugar instead, since naked cakes are *so* chic – because, as always, the more precise you have to be, the more numbers you're going to see.

Tiers

See how the number of tiers went down with the design just then? You've probably noticed by now that more cake = more money. If you don't want to trim your guest list, serve the sweet, pretty thing as dessert so you're not required to account for the evening guests too. It's not mean, just practical – they've got a barbecue or a sweetie table coming, right?

Another way *round* it – see what I did there? – is to go for a square. Any baker worth her vanilla essence will tell you you'll get more slices from a square or rectangular confection than you would from the regular circle. Try to avoid bizarre shapes too – the more awkward to bake or put together, the more time it will take, and the more it's going to cost you.

None of this working for you? Then I'll let you in on a trick of the trade: have your baker make and basically ice as many tiers as you need, but only ask them to *decorate* and *display* two or three. You'll be surprised how often plain extra/back-up tiers are kept in the kitchen, then cut up and served with the rest of cake, and no-one's any the wiser. It won't save you as much as any of the other options, but hey, at least it'll take the edge off.

Type

It's the same basic rule: the harder to do/more expensive/ more unusual something is, the more it's going to pile on the payments. If your baker has to source a specific cognac for your boozy filling from way out who-knows-where you're likely to get the bill for the time and postage. If you want a fragile cake that has to be set slowly and carefully, and transported tentatively, that's all the time they could have spent doing someone else's dessert.

Talk types and flavours with your baker – fruit, sponge, chocolate, carrot, cheese, chiffon, ginger, lemon, Madeira, ice-cream etc. etc. etc. – and see if you can't come to an agreement that balances the books.

Best for: Karma points, obviously (think of the happy, smiling faces of your local baker's little family) – and low budget brides who are after something a little less off-the-shelf.

At Grandma's Knee

When was the last time you went round your nan's? I'm serious. I haven't seen my remaining nana in more than a year and I hold my hands up: it's on me. She's more of a cook than a baker – my gran was the bow-to-her-prowess cake-crafter – but if your family matriarch has or even once had the whisking skills of a cement mixer, why not call in her expertise either to make your cake or to show you how?

She doesn't have to be able to decorate it too – we'll cover that in a minute – and of course this isn't limited to nannas if Granddad's really the man for the job (or your mum or your best friend or your second cousin twice-removed for that matter). The point is that if you can draft someone in who's been angling to help, or make them feel useful and their cakes appreciated, where's the harm? Plus it takes another thing effortlessly off your plate – and, y'know, onto a nice cake stand.

Best for: Barely-there-budget brides, and themes that need that old-school, not-quite-perfect, handmade look.

Shop-Bought Beauties

Elaborate cakes by the big bakers can set you back hundreds – in the case of the most completely crazy creations, even a thousand or more – and yes, for that kind of currency you'd expect to see and taste the difference.

But there are other ways to have a super-slick big-day cake without the cost – whether it's three flower-covered tiers made to your precise specifications, or some plain white ones you picked up at the supermarket and decked out with your own, um, decs.

Marks & Spencer

These aren't just cakes. They're M&S cakes. And they're M&S prices – compare with the quote from your baker before you assume they're a better bet. But next to a lot of the fanciest sponge-structures out there, many styles are more than reasonable: at the time of writing you could build your own sponge or all-butter fruit cake, with tiny tiers starting from £8 or XL from £44. Alternatively, a trad white trio-tier with pearly finish and matching ribbons came out at £179, or a seriously cool two-tier fruitcake covered in edible flowers was £75. It's not just the classic white-iced variety, either: there were contemporary cakes served upside down – yes, that's biggest tier on top (£229) – and chocolate cakes surrounded by cocoa-y cigarillos (£249).

Supermarket Sweep

Depending on the time of year, big boys such as Sainsbury's often stock simple, undecorated fruit or sponge cakes with basic white icing. They're not always available in several sizes, but there's no rule that says they have to be served up in a stack – check out the Alternatives section for other display options, and Baking & Decorating for ways to beautify your cake.

Waitrose

If even just a little bit of you wants to be a princess on your W-day, it's probably worth knowing that Fiona Cairns made the wedding cakes for William and Catherine. Funny I should mention that, since she's also been doing the same fine work for Waitrose for the last 20 years – which means we can get our commoners' mitts on food that's literally fit for the Queen.

I've seen one of Fiona's undecorated, three-tier wedding cakes go for £210, so not the least expensive on our list – but did I mention she made lovely layers that were probably munched on by Prince Harry? If you're going for a more intimate do, your choice tends to be a bit broader – I've spied the likes of a heart-shaped cake covered in red, pink and orange petals to serve 20 – 30 for £59, or the same for 40 – 50 people for £69.

Best for: Low-budget brides looking for something plain and simple to deck out themselves, or the traditional fairy-tale confection without the 'you're-dreaming' price tag.

Alternatives

Fight the power! The wedding cake may be a time-honoured tradition, but if your only reason for having it is that everyone else does, look out for that cliff coming up. I say it's about time we stood up and let our tiers be counted, because some of us don't want the fancy white number, and some of us – whisper it – don't even *like* cake.

Hey There, Good Looking

It's not what you do, it's the way that you do it… Can't find three cakes of three different sizes to stack on top of each other? Rather have three different flavours for equal numbers of people? Obsessed with a light and fluffy cake that won't take the other layers' weight? Go for what you want – just give your display tactics some thought.

My favourite way to work it is with separate cake stands in complementary colours – pastel pink, yellow and green, for instance – or glass pedestals with covers for a flourish before the photos.

Cheese, Glorious Cheese

Brie, Cheddar and Stilton! This is a popular one with savoury types who'd rather order the board than the pud when they eat out: not a cheesecake in the traditional New York, sweet, soft sense, but a stack of blocks of your favourite savoury flavours styled in the shape of a wedding cake.

John Lewis does a lovely selection by The Fine Cheese Co. that you can expect to pay around £140 to £360 for. The least expensive I've seen featured four tiers: Langres, Jean Grogne, Tomme de Savoie and Cornish Yarg; and the most boasted five: White Nancy, Jean Grogne, Dorset Blue Vinny, Cornish Yarg and Keen's Cheddar.

Marks & Sparks had two options for the cheesily-inclined at last glance: a smaller five-tier structure made of Gould's Cheddar, Lancashire, white Stilton and cranberry, Brie, and Blacksticks Blue Truckle (£89); or a chunkier five-tier concoction of Gould's cheddar, Farmhouse Red Leicester, Farmhouse Double Gloucester, Blacksticks Blue, and Raven's Oak goat's cheese (£155).

Waitrose didn't let us down with their gourmet triplet at the same time either: think three tiers of Petit Basque, Cashel Blue and Appleby's Farmhouse Cheshire for £70; three of Cornish Yarg, Cropwell Bishop Stilton and Hafod Welsh Cheddar for £110; or four of Cashel Blue, Manchego, Hafod Welsh Cheddar and Sparkenhoe Red Leicester for £200.

Of course, this is one of the easiest ones to do at home as long as you've got a knife and either a chopping board display base or a cake stand – just ensure your toughest types of cheese hold the fort at the bottom, while the softer sorts remain topside. You could even pick up your slabs direct from a local farm, then serve your cheesy colossus with a selection of fruits for pairing, *Ratatouille*-style.

Stateside Sweethearts

They came, we tasted, they conquered – the American cupcake is quickly climbing the ranks to become one of Wedding World's favourite alternative desserts. And don't think your local supermarket hasn't noticed.

One way forward is to pick up a multipack straight from the bakery or off the shelf, but if you prefer something a little more bespoke, that's in the hands of the usual suspects – and the prices next to your trad cake are impressive.

Marks & Spencer have been known to do a choice of mini or full-size cupcakes – I'd recommend the littlies as part of a sweetie table, but go with the bigger ones in lieu of a cake. You could get 48 vanilla or strawberry cupcakes for £48 last time I checked – I'll let you do the maths per person.

As for **Waitrose**, their cupcakes were again by one of baking's queen bees: that royally rated Fiona Cairns. I've seen delicate little lovelies finely decorated with petals work out at £1.08 each when sold in batches of 12. Alternatively, vintage fairytale cupcakes with much more dainty detail were £22 for 12 – £1.83 each. (Sidenote: these didn't coming up under the 'cupcakes' section on the site, but were worth a scroll through the main cakes.)

Don't assume the prices at your local bakery/cupcakery are prohibitive though. Just because their creations come out at £2.50 each when you sneak a treat for yourself doesn't mean they won't be willing to negotiate if you buy in bulk.

Wonder Wobbles

If you think gourmet jelly sounds like an oxymoron, go to jellymongers.co.uk and get some inspiration from Bompass & Parr. They also do a book that details how to make everything from cocktail-flavoured concoctions to glow-in-the-dark wobblers.

Get your moulds from the likes of **Amazon**, **Lakeland**, **notonthehighstreet.com** and some of the other bizarre-cooking stars in the Baking and Decorating section (below).

Dough for Dough

Profiteroles, macarons – even donuts. If it can be stacked up in pretty piles or crafted into a croquembouche, anything goes on your W-day. Hop to it yourself or talk to your local baker about that special pudding that you and hubby-to-be have happy memories of.

Want something more savoury? Try your taste buds at a pork pie cake. **Wilsons Butchers** have been known to whip one up that serves 100 people for about £120.

Best for: Mini-budget brides who aren't so kitchen-savvy, or want something with the wow-factor to make their day feel different.

Bride Power

Rather take this one for the team and get your very own bake on? Then I'd advise choosing a type of cake that lasts longer than a day or so for starters (you don't want to be spreading buttercream at the same time as getting your hair put up) and one that's sturdy enough to take the weight of pillars and extra layers if needs be.

You might also want to consider having a back-up plan in the works, like a shop-bought cake you can wheel out so you don't call the whole thing off in frustration when the bottom layer collapses at three in the morning. But if you're serious about this – and you're head-on-straight enough to handle it – then here are a few places you might find handy recipes.

Baking Blogs

There are tonnes of good ones out there – have a Google, have a play. Just make sure you do it way in advance of your day. Anything that has open comments or recipe reviews is handy and can help point you in the direction of the ones that work, but there's no substitute for apron-ing up and getting stuck in.

For my money (or lack of it), I'd spend some time on **Punchfork** – these days a part of Pinterest – where I've dug up Mexican pistachio wedding cakes along with the usual when I searched

142

for, well, the usual. Better to flick through until you find an unrelated recipe that resonates with you – Valentine sorbet sandwiches (thanks, Martha Stewart), Neapolitan cupcakes (cheers, My Baking Addiction) or spicy apple-butter BBQ pork cupcakes (yes, you read that right – courtesy of Doughmesstic), anyone? Said recipe duly found, check out what the same poster has got of the cakey variety and modify to taste.

Baking Books

Can't afford a couture creation by your most beloved baker? Buy their book and recreate the recipe at home. Some big titles by some of the hostesses with the mostess(es?) include: *Romantic Cakes* by Peggy Porschen, *Chic & Unique Wedding Cakes* by Zoe Clark and *Bake & Decorate* by Fiona Cairns.

Alternatively, if you're a bit of a baking buff already, you probably pick up the odd cake-making/decorating magazine. Look out for the big names in the bylines, since the masters often lend them their expertise.

Best for: Mini-budget brides with the baking nous to navigate a recipe – and who have the time and pennies for supplies so they can practise a few times.

Baking & Decorating

Not sure where to find blue chocolate dye, a cake topper of two arctic foxes tying the knot or a jelly mould in the shape of an anatomical heart? MakeBake.co.uk, Etsy and Amazon respectively, as it turns out. And there's more of the sweet and the scary where that little lot came from – if you don't want to ask your florist for an extra cake-topping arrangement, that is…

Amazon

Is there anything they *don't* do? Last time I was on there my search-engine rampage couldn't even stump them with a train-shaped jelly mould (£2.99, The Magic Toy Shop). They might not be great for the more obscure cooking ingredients but you'll be surprised how many off-the-wall additions they do have – better, though, as a place for the likes of affordable wedding cake toppers and cake stands.

Cubicuk.com

I don't normally do this, but, I just feel like we have this kind of connection… Me and Cubicuk, that is. Because I'm not usually a novelty-shop kinda girl, but there's something edgy and *actually* funny about the oddball odds and sods at this weirdly wonderful online shop. In the past I've come across a box of four plastic crowns to serve cupcakes in for £12.50 – or the robotic equivalent for £14.95 (search: 'Yum Bots'). But the real goodie that I want for my own has to be the cake candelabra – yes, you read that right – that was going for just £5.95.

Debenhams

Besides the fact that I love everything Tala ever made and most of it's sold at Debenhams, they're also a surprisingly good bet for the more cost-effective end of pretty essentials – like the 250 super-cute fairy cake cases in Cath Kidston-wannabe patterns that I spotted for £7.50. If you're determined to do the generally pricier silicone muffin cases, they can be competitive here too – I've seen a six-pack of pretty, round pastel ones for £8.50, or you could get 12 star-shaped versions for a sweet £7.50. There was also the occasional unusual necessity, like the rarely-seen-in-the-wilds-of-department-stores cake-pop baking mould for just £10.

Dotcomgiftshop

If you like your bakes vintage or quirky, this is the place to be. Give you a for-instance? Alright: they've stocked cake cases covered in London buses and Buckingham palace guards for £1.50 for 60, a 60-pack of cake cases decorated with tiny woodland mushrooms for £1.50 and a 30cm white cake stand with laser-cut lovebirds for £11.95. See what I mean?

Etsy

Are you after something you think only exists in your dreams? They're about to come true at Etsy. Digging through the virtual treasure trove I've found a silicone mould that makes vintage-style cameos from moldsrus for $6.95 (about £4.50), as well as a pair of clay wedding ninjas – yes, the stealthy, kick-ass kind – from Lilley to top your cake with for £12. Proof, if you needed it, that Etsy is a place where you can get nearly anything – as long as you know what you want.

There's a lot of trawling involved unless you have some specific ideas that translate to effective search terms. Typing in 'wedding cake topper' I got 19,119 items, while 'dragon wedding cake toppers' took it down to 27 (from £5.18 to £126.03). Be strategic and they could be a goldmine for personalising your bakes – as well as the ceramics you present them on.

Folksy

Like Etsy's Brit-only brethren, they're a hotspot for handmade pretty and witty crafts that hail from our fair shores. At the time of writing that meant everything from robin bride and groom cake toppers (£10, Amys clay critters) to pretty vintage, mismatched cake stands (£25 to £35, For alice with love; or £24.99, Vintage table), as well as a good line in stands made of recycled records (£12.99, Vinyl wall).

Hobbycraft

It's not all paints and art supplies over at Hobbycraft – the DIY extraordinaires have branched out into baking in a big way. I've seen them stock everything from flower-shaped Wilton wraps for cake pops (£2.99 for eight) and a 23-piece Hilly's Kitchen wire cupcake stand (£6.99) to my personal biggie: a Wilton pan set that lets you make a cake with a heart running through the middle (£22.99) – cue the big reveal at cutting time!

IncrEDIBLE Toppers
Technically they're an Etsy shop, but they're more deserving of their own headline – especially if you're wondering how on earth you're meant to make your own cascade of beautiful butterflies. I spotted a 25-pack in all the colours of the rainbow for $15 (£9.73).

John Lewis
See, the problem with John Lewis is that they sell Tala *and* Hope and Greenwood, which basically means I'd better wait outside while you go in. If you can resist temptation, though, trust me – you *will* be rewarded. In the past, said prizes have included Something in the Air lacework cupcake wraps (10 for £6.50), pretty silicone moulds in 12-packs of circles, hearts and stars (from £6 to £9) and 500ml jelly moulds (£3).

Lakeland
Cake magazine eds love a bit of Lakeland, and you've got to hand it to them: the creative kitchenware people certainly do know what they're talking about. From dessert moulds (£2.49) to blackbird pie funnels (£2.49) via ready-to-roll red icing (£1.49), heart-shaped icing cutters (£2.99) and ornate cake stencils for that vintage finish (£5.99), they've always been the perfect place to pick up those bits and bobs that make your job as cake artiste easier.

MakeBake.co.uk
Ready to get seriously stuck in and go all advanced-baker on me? Wrap chocolate printed with vintage flowers round your cakes for about £2.80 a sheet, get on board with retro-style cake push pops – which are exactly as exciting as they sound! – for around

£39.98 or just pick out a super-cute cake-wrap kit from roughly £3.98. This is the place for everything weird and wonderful you've ever heard of in baking – and a few easy cheats to get the same results for half the hassle.

Notonthehighstreet.com

Toppers and cake stands and decs, oh my! It's all at notonthehigh-street – especially if you want it with a quirky or vintage bent. My top picks last time I was there? Stackable floral cake tins in three sizes (£16.95 from This is Pretty, The Chic Country Home or The Rose Shack) or a three-tier, ceramic cake stand threaded with ribbon (£20, The Orchard).

Squires Kitchen

After more kitchen wizardry in the way of sugarcraft kits, pastes, ganache or fully-formed chocolate roses? Maybe you'd prefer a pillar for your layer cake (expect to pay about £5.30 each) or a Disney Princess figurine to stand on top (about £4.99)? Whatever pretty, sparkly or elegant bits and pieces you need to fill or finish your concoctions, SK has something tucked away for even the most discerning dessert designer.

Williams-Sonoma

They do everything from fancy-pants bakeware (Le Creuset? Don't *maaand* if ah *dooo*) to Nordic Ware aluminium bundt pans that I've seen priced at £25.72 (is it just me, or could you use that to make giant rose-shaped jellies?). But my favourite bit has to be their did-I-really-just-see-that? decorations – if you ever had a sticker- or badge-maker as a kid, prepare for the personalised embosser (was £29.40).

Best for: DIY brides who want to make something spectacular from scratch, or not-so-crafty types looking to cut a few corners but still end up with a beautiful bake.

Hire

Just another reason to get in with your local baker: many will hire out cake stands for half the price (or less) of buying – order your cake there and they might even chuck one in for free.

I wish I could list a bazillion places here, but since most cakeries don't post their fragile wares (in-person pick-up only), many would only suit certain readers. Better to buddy-up and make your own local cake-making pal-o'-mine.

Unless, that is, you're looking to hire a helluva lot more crockery – in which case take a peek at the Hire list in the upcoming Style Details chapter.

Best for: Barely-there-budget brides, or ones without the room for a collection of cake stands after the day.

CHAPTER 11

The Flowers

Blooming good deals on everything from bouquets to buttonholes

If you ever go on Mastermind, do you know what your specialist subject's going to be? Flowers. It's going to be flowers. Not anything you ever learned in school, anything you ever read or saw on TV, or anything you, y'know, studied for three years at uni. Because the encyclopaedic knowledge of flowers you're about to garner from planning your wedding is going to push all sorts of essential information out of your brain. You may never tie your own shoelaces again.

Before You Start

Try saying this to any married woman if she looks like she could do with a laugh: 'It's just a few bouquets, right – how much could it be?' Because flowers are the thing that is easiest to underestimate – in terms of both abundance and cost.

You'll need to be strategic, and you'll need to know your stuff – via your local florist, some crafty Googling or a trip to the library, whichever works for you – if you're going to keep your floral total from blooming out of control.

Punches in Bunches

I know you know it's not just a few bouquets, but even I struggle to keep in my head how many flowery options there are on your wedding day. Buttonholes, pomanders, pew ends, table centres, chair backs, corsages, cake tops, pedestal displays, even arches – you point to it, and your florist will cover it in petals. Speaking of which, you're probably going to need some confetti – unless you're going old-school and getting everyone to bring a handful of their own.

Anyway, decide how many of these things are important to you right now. Because it's the usual shtick if you're getting someone else to sort them: the more you have, the more complex they are and the longer it'll take to pull them together, the more they're going to cost you. And even if you're arranging them yourself, you'll still need to buy the blooms.

Do your groom and best men *need* buttonholes when they can hire a pocket square with their suit? Do you want flowers on the tables *as well as* those giant, vintage candelabra? And can't you take the pew ends from the ceremony and use them on chair backs at the reception? Recycling your flowers from one venue to the next is one of the savviest ways to save some pennies.

'Tis the Season

However many flowers you have, have ones that are in season and preferably local – they're more abundant, easier to source and therefore cheaper. If you're not sure which will be around at the time of your wedding, ask your florist or Google it before you settle on anything.

Filler Florals

If you're determined to go off-season or you're head over heels for the big daddies of romance – roses, lilies or orchids, for instance – there are two ways to keep the prices in the seedling stage. First up: downsize your arrangements – the fewer blooms, the better. Second: pad them out with big, statement flowers that aren't as expensive – I love ranunculus and peonies, personally – or go for a good handful of greenery.

A Flower-Finding Mission

There are plenty of ways to track down your flowers – and they all have their own pluses and minuses. Some come with tinier price tags but push up your need-to-knows. Others tack on labour costs but guarantee a pro finish. And some just require some elbow grease and a touch of talent that you didn't even know you had.

The Traditional Way

For starters, you could ask your florist. That's right – your little local florist with her tiny shop squished in-between Costa and Halfords that has those big potted trees outside that you always trip over. *Her. She* knows about flowers already, and she wants to help you out in a big, *big* way, because you're never likely to need so many flowers at once again.

But that doesn't mean you have to give her a month's salary. In fact, she can help you spend *less* – she knows which flowers are in season and aren't, which ones she can pick up locally, which ones keep on opening throughout your day (tulips, for starters) and which ones need to be kept refrigerated until the very last minute to save them from drooping. And you're not the only bride on a budget she's ever helped out either, so she can suggest the best blooms to come in under yours.

Best for: Perfectionistas – no-one does a faultless finish quite like someone who's been tying ribbons round flowers for the last 10 years. Also organised brides who like to have everything down, months in advance.

Supermarkets

I don't know about you, but the last place I picked up a bouquet was Morrisons, and it didn't cost more than a fiver. If you're keeping your flowers minimal and just need a few for the bouquets and/or table centres, your local megastore could be a good bet.

Styles vary from traditional and countrified to simpler and more modern, so there's no need to settle for less than chic – but timing issues mean this isn't one for the faint-hearted, super-organised or oh-so-perfect bride.

The number one rule here is to check your delivery details – at the time of writing ASDA was offering delivery dates as far out as three weeks – because you won't want to tangle with suppliers who *can't guarantee* a named date. Also, be aware that bouquets will change with the season – the flowers that were spot-on in spring might not be around at all in autumn.

Best for: Whirlwind weddings. No time to waste and an eager pack of maids on speed dial? Delegate the ones with a stylistic eye you trust to place the orders for you.

Grow Your Own
Well, not *you*, exactly – unless you've got plenty of time and are happy to plan ahead and be prepared if your shoots don't come through. But maybe your gran keeps a lovely rose garden, or your dad still spends his Saturdays at the allotment? If keen relatives have friends in floral places, draft them in to provide the raw materials for your grand designs.

Pick Your Own
No such luck? Then do your local farmers some good – many will offer a pick-your-own service akin to strawbs or similar. Some will even arrange your flowers for you and deliver them on the day if you're willing to go with a colour scheme rather than specific species.

Wholesale
If you just *have* to have that special exotic bloom that's neither in season nor from our shores and it's going to cost too much to

source from your sweet-ol-lady florist, there is the option to cut out the middle man and go direct to online wholesalers. Just be sure to check their reviews and maybe order a smaller number of samples first – that way you can check the service and merchandise ahead of time, and you'll quickly find out if they have minimum orders.

Best for: This cheery trio are spot-on for DIY brides who have arranging their own blossoms on their mind. Just be sure to practise plenty beforehand…

Fake it to Make It

No opening, wilting or staining to worry about, *and* they're more likely to survive the trip from one venue to the next? Faux flowers are the way to go for blooms without the stress. The artificial stuff is available online from sites like **bloom.uk.com** and **dunelm-mill. com** as well as a whole line of wholesalers – and that's before we even get to all the gardening and homeware shops. At the time of writing you could even pick them up at your local **Wilkinson**, along with floral tape and dri-foam.

Best for: Hassle-free flowers or blooms galore in winter – also a bridal bouquet that lasts forever. If you're getting them online though, as always, order one or two to start with and run your own quality check.

Tricks of the Trade

There's a bit more to flower arranging than jamming as many stems as you can into a vase. If you're going to go your own way, here are some handy ways to ratchet up your know-how.

Classes

Florists big and small do them, from two-hour sessions concentrating on bouquets to whole days – heck, weeks if a new career direction is on the cards. The thing to do is weigh the benefits of face-to-face tuition against the cost of lessons on top of buying your own flowers. And shop around – a lot of florists are independent, so class prices can vary enormously.

Got a whole gaggle of eager helpers? Going as a group may save on the price per head, but sending a representative who can then teach you all is generally a more cost-effective way forward.

Best for: Low-budget, hands-on brides who'd rather get stuck in than spend ages reading, trawling and training. Also attention-to-detail types who want to achieve you-did-that-*yourself?* perfection.

Online

Ah YouTube, you mecca of niche skills, useless information and cats getting sat on by babies. Here you can play, pause and practise your flower-arranging prowess at your own pace – often with the on-screen guidance of some pretty talented florists. Try **MarthaStewart**, **videojugartscrafts** and **HowdiniGuru** and go from there.

Best for: Barely-there-budget brides who learn best by watching, but have little cash or want to up their skills at anti-social times.

Books

There are all manner of books and eBooks on the subject, and I'll be honest – I haven't read most of them. If I were you, I'd flick through a few in your local bookshop or preview on Amazon and the like, as well as reading as many reviews as you can get hold of before you buy. The last thing you want is to spend your hard-earned cash-money hand over fist on the information you need to even get started.

Best for: Mini-budget brides who want to take their time, step away from a screen and keep learning costs down. Also step-by-step types who prefer a recipe to a cooking show.

Alternatives

Whether you just want to put your flowers on display in an unusual way or you've never really been the petal-picking type, here are some alternatives to the traditional vase-and-urn brigade.

Displays with a Difference

What you put your flowers in is going to depend on the feel of your day as well as your budget. For **low-cost vintage-style or rustic looks**, collect plant pots, teacups, teapots, jam jars, pretty watering cans or even wellington boots. Fill with individual, open buds or haphazard snatches of English blooms that look like you nonchalantly plucked them off a country path.

For **inexpensive modern chic**, think statement flowers with the beauty or sheer size to stand alone. Twist single-stem orchids, lilies, roses or birds of paradise around the inside of fishbowls, or slip them individually into tall, slender glasses or vases. Alternatively, really keep things on the right side of your price bracket: cut peonies or ranunculus short and float them in stumpy tumblers or stone or glass bowls. For a twist of decadent glamour, thoroughly clean out pretty perfume bottles and use as vases for trimmer stems.

For a **retro feel**, do what we did: collect coffee jars (hands up: some of them were Dolmio jars), glass Diet Coke bottles and pretty pink lemonade or wine bottles. Strip off the paper, rinse and fill with just a few stems each for a cheaper, more inventive alternative to one big, bloom-stuffed bouquet.

Online, find everything you need at sites like **eBay** – which can help with the hoards of second-hand, old-school items – or **Etsy, Folksy** and co. In the flesh, try supermarkets, antique shops, pound stores or even the likes of good old **Wilko** (about £3 for a small teal vase or £2.75 for a jam jar, anyone?) or **TK Maxx**.

Homespun Sweetness

A sprig of herb makes a simple, fragrant replacement for a button-hole. Fabric hearts stitched with your initials and hung on ribbon make for pretty pew ends and chair backs (get your kit on at Hobbycraft). Swap table centres for cake pops, lollies poked into spheres of dri-foam or stacks of your favourite old paperbacks tied with ribbon or twine.

See the Light

Whether it's table centres or decs, pew ends or pedestal displays, **lighting is romantic enough to replace fresh flowers** and it can often come out cheaper. Choose tall candlebra instead of pedestal arrangements; twists or meshes of fairy lights instead of pew ends or for general ambience; and tea lights floating in water or scattered on tables instead of centrepieces. Nod to your theme with rustic, vintage, or exquisitely simple holders and containers picked up at the usual suspects from the Displays with a Difference section.

Best for: Days with a specific theme or brides with a penchant for the quirky or surprising.

CHAPTER 12

The Entertainment

All that jazz... but not for all those pennies

Let meeee entertain you... with all you need to know about keeping your groupies happy long after the cake and toasting wine have dried up. 'Cause unless you're planning on skipping out early, jetting off on your honeymoon and leaving your guests with nothing to do except the clearing up, there's this little thing called fun I'm guessing you want to cram the whole night with. Whether you're thinking DJ, band or something a bit more off-the-wall, here's how to keep your entertainment costs lower than your nan can limbo.

Before You Start

I'm not going to tell you not to have a DJ or a band (although a DJ is generally the cheaper of the two, if you were wondering), but you will find a whole bunch of alternatives coming up. If you can't imagine your wedding without your dad's dancing or your sister flirting with the drummer though, here's how to make it work without it costing you a pretty penny.

Time

The earlier you bring on your act, the longer they'll need to hang around, and the later they stay, the more the chance you'll need to feed them. Work out whether the extra hours or the extra heads on the buffet will cost you more (likely the hours) and sacrifice whichever you're happier to give up.

When it comes to sussing out the timings of everything from the ceremony to the wedding brekkie and beyond, consider slotting your performers in for an hour or two rather than all night, and fill the rest of the time with one of the alternative, cheaper options below.

Place

This isn't just me giving it some more of the local love: hire entertainers that live nearby and it could save you on all sorts. First up, many expect you to pay their travel if it's outside a certain radius; second, depending on how far away from home they are, others might even want you to put them up. If you're dead-set on someone from outside the area, definitely be sure to check these extra fees out first.

The VIP Treatment

That's Venue In Progress – while you're looking into booking your reception, remember to ask if they have recommended suppliers. For one thing, it'll add to your options if you're not sure where to start, and for another, they might have a discount agreement going with DJs and bands they book a lot.

A Cheap Night Out

Before you lay down the cold, hard cash, make sure you see your players in action. Call or meet them and explain that you've heard good things and are really interested – if you've got the negotiating skills you may be able to wangle a discounted or comp ticket to see them live before you sign anything. Now *that's* the kind of wedding planning we can all get on board with.

The Boy in the Band

If even limiting the timeframe and the distance leaves you too lacking in the cash department, consider the old faithfuls – bring in a friend, or some making-a-name-for-themselves newcomers. Your pals will be more than happy to sort you out free-gratis, while students or bands might give you a discount for the captive audience and the chance to make new fans. Either way, go and see them before you put it to them – it saves red faces if they turn out not to actually be your thang.

Best for: Trad receptions that start with *Puppy Love* and end with *I'm Gonna Be (500 Miles)*. Also cool music-loving types who want to showcase their taste in jazz or, y'know, bluegrass.

Alternatives

Don't fancy bopping to Hanson all night or watching your brother trying to teach your gramps to headbang? Or maybe that's exactly what you had in mind but your penny-pot just won't stretch that far. Music, magic or something a bit spectacular – you'll find a plan to keep you and yours amused among these oddball alternatives.

Hook Me Up

Your iPod, that is. Because no-one's looking at the DJ while they're rocking out – and *your* playlist means back-to-back music you love. There's a trend for asking guests to submit their favourite song with their RSVP so you can guarantee there's a tune on there for everyone – and trust me, it was a giggle seeing what tunes everyone picked for our big day. Just be sure to ask your venue if they've got a suitable sound system – you'll be surprised by how many restaurants and unexpected spots have got you covered.

Garden Games

Going with a marquee or somewhere with an outdoor area? Buy or even hire some outdoor games – think giant chess or Jenga. Set them up in the morning and guests can keep busy during the photos – they're even better when evenings are lighter for longer in the summer.

Alternatively, sports fans can rent or supply the kit for matches. Get friends and family competing at cricket, rounders or even croquet – or keep the costs down with a good old game of five-a-side.

Hit the Deck

If your guest list is a little on the octogenarian side, chances are the dance floor won't be filled until the wee hours – but that doesn't necessarily mean it's past your elders' bedtimes. A pack of cards on every table is a cheap and simple way to bring the fun once feet have given in.

Karaoke

Go on, you know you want to. Maybe not for the *whole* night, but post-band/DJ when everybody's drunk enough. All you need is some basic AV equipment and a tried-and-tested karaoke DVD. Or you could even ask your venue if you can plug in your games console and SingStar the night away.

Picture This

Hiring a photo booth might be out of your price range, but it's super-simple and affordable to set one up yourself. Polaroids are back in fashion so you can pick up the relevant camera, or just use the digital one you already have. Suspend a frame from the ceiling if you can, or set it up on a table for people to pick up and pose through using the props you provide. Expect a guest book or SD card packed with your pals posing in rainbow wigs, oversized plastic glasses and feather boas – or something more themed/elegant if that's the way you want to go.

Quiz

Whether they admit it or not, everybody loves a pub quiz. Especially if the prizes include a crate of alcohol and some sweet treats. If you're worried some guests won't get picked for teams, you can either play by your table plan or leave an envelope on each one with a list of the players who should sit there. It's a fun way to mingle, and let's be honest – every family's got a born compère.

Silhouettes & Sketches
Maybe your mum's always going on about your cousin Andy's art skills. Or maybe there's a college or uni nearby where you could advertise for someone who's got the talent. Because the latest thing at oh-so-fancy affairs is to have a silhouette artist draw and cut out your guests in a flash right in front of them (could make a lovely guest book, or personalised favours). Then there's the less ooh-la-la alternative: a quick-draw cartoon-style sketch artist.

Voilà!
There's nothing like a bit of childish amazement – especially when it's written across your auntie's face. Whether it's for the kids or the grown-ups, close-up magicians can work wonders at intimate venues.

Best for: Mishmash nights – maybe you can't afford eight hours of band/DJ-ing, or maybe your families are a melting pot of styles and tastes. Also intimate venues that don't have the room for a dance floor or dance floor *and* band.

CHAPTER 13

The Photography

Happy snaps at prices to smile about

Ah, the photos. There are the obligatory ones of your dress on the hanger and your shoes with the toes artistically pointed together; you grinning your head off at the altar and the moment confetti went in your eye on the venue steps; the truly, madly, deeply happy smiles and the genuinely awkward 'sexy' embrace. And that's all before your photographer clambers up a tree to get the traditional 'cheese!' from up above.

Whatever shots you've got in mind and however you imagine your album – full of pensive black and white, lively bright colour or that nostalgic vintage tint – you *can* have your dream album without your nightmare price tag, as long as you're willing to be flexible on a few things.

Before You Start
It's a risky business skimping on your snapper, but if you really can't afford anyone too flash, there are ways and means of finding not-so-official alternatives coming up. If you'd rather not chance it

162

on pictures you'll be showing to your grandkids though, here are a few tricks to keep your pro-picture budget as low as it can go.

The Hours
As with any supplier, the longer your photographer hangs around, the more hours you'll be billed for, and the more likely you'll also have to pay to feed them while they're there. Think long and hard about the big-day memories that matter most to you – or the ones you'd rather keep to yourselves if it makes cutting the camera-time easier.

Maybe you want to capture the exact moment your hair becomes a sparkly two-foot beehive, or perhaps you'd prefer the hectic backstage moments with your bridesmaids to be off-limits. The 'I do's are almost certainly on everybody's pic-list, but do you really want a lifelong record of how dishevelled everyone got after the first dance? Identify your ideal window – when you want those perfect pics – and outside that, have a maid on hand with a digital camera for rough-and-ready snaps.

Where, Oh Where?
I know 'go local' is my mantra, but there's an extra bridal bonus when it comes to your photographer: you may be expected to pay for travel outside a certain radius, while really far-out photo-takers might even want you to put them up. I'd opt for the sharp-shooter who lives a lot nearer if you don't want to shell out the extra costs.

Digital Love
I warn you now: many pros don't do discs or USBs of their photos – they tend to keep the copyright so they can charge for extra prints. But if your snapper understands your financial situation, try negotiating: either explain that the disc is all you can afford, or agree a number of prints that you're willing to pay for, then top it up with a shortlist that's supplied on-disc and copyright-free.

Second in Command

We found our photographer via, well, another photographer – she wasn't willing to bring down her own price, but the girl who'd been her second was striking out on her own. A couple of emails later we'd gone from the £1,600 never-gonna-happen snapper to her £500 breakout star – and because they'd worked together, their styles were super-similar.

My top tip: find the pro whose pics you love, and to begin with, negotiate direct. Photographers get their names out there through mag and blog coverage, and they get *that* by shooting unusual weddings with lots of personal details. Take the time to describe your day and it could help you swing a discount – but be sure to mention other persuasion points, like your wedding being off-season or midweek. The less likely they are to already be or to become booked up, the more moolah you're likely to save.

If that doesn't work out – and trust me, we were offered cuts of as much as 50% for our winter wedding – don't be shy about asking for recommendations of other lens-lovers who are more in your price range. Many photographers know others in their industry, or work with a second whose figures are waaaay less fanciful.

Best for: Utterly dreamy photos that keep their charm as years go by. Also, effortless sourcing without all the extra legwork.

Other Ways with Wedding Pics

Personally, I'm all for signing on with a pro without stumping up the max, but it's not always easy to afford the full-on flashbulb-and-tripod treatment. If your photo budget's a bit on the slim side, here are some alternative ways to get your big day on (virtual) film.

Friend of the Family

An oldie but a goodie, there's always the option to draft in the family photo-fan. The only issue is making sure Uncle Mike's not too arty, or that Auntie Elle doesn't get distracted. The key here is to pick someone who not only knows their flash from their focus, but understands what you want and won't use family status to justify poor quality.

Best for: Barely-there-budget brides and grooms, especially if you've got truly talented relatives who want to give you an alternative wedding gift. The pluses: you'll save cash and could feel instantly at ease with them. The minuses: family fracas if your pics aren't what you want.

Fresh & Flash
Student photographers are an option – consider advertising on a noticeboard or in the uni paper – but you'll need to make sure they're sorted by your wedding insurance, or else take out coverage separately. Why? In case they lose your photos or your cousin collides with their lighting kit. Most pros already have their very own super-shiny insurance policies.

A better option might be a new start-up business that's looking to pump up their portfolio – they should be switched on to camerawork, insurance and such but not yet have the shots to show for it. Find these via Google, ads on wedding websites, posting on relevant message boards *or* by asking established photographers (see Second in Command, above). Often they're looking for their first few weddings and will do yours at a discount.

Whoever you go with, always make sure you get a taste of their skillset first. For us that was as simple as meeting our snapper face-to-face, getting a feel for her personality and having a flick through her iPad portfolio but if you want to make triple-sure, see if they'll give you an hour-long engagement shoot at a discount. That way you can get a feel for their style and get comfy in front of their camera, as well as working out how each of you sees the shots going on your W-day.

Best for: Mini-budget brides and grooms who are willing to take a chance on a fresh talent. You never know, you might even find yourselves the next big thing!

Fill in the Gaps

If you can only afford the big guns for a fleeting window, fill in early-morning and post-wedding-breakfast photos in the following ways. I'm not going to kid you: they won't be the same standard as your snapper's super-shots, but it's better than letting those special memories completely fade away.

First up: your bezzies' smartphones. Encourage your maids to get snapping for some fun shots of your pre-aisle antics – than add a filter in Instagram or Camera+, or have the real bright sparks go get their Photoshop on.

Second: disposables on your guests' tables. Buy these in bulk from places like **confetti.co.uk**, where I've seen 10 – 249 cameras in the colour of your choice go for as little as £1.99 each. Attach a note asking guests to put each camera in a colourful bucket or basket you've supplied on their way out, or leaving instructions if you're happy to have them posted or scanned and uploaded to Facebook. Just don't forget, if you keep hold of the cameras, you'll have to pay to have your pictures printed.

Third: you may have spotted this in Entertainment – it's a personal favourite: mock up your own photo booth complete with digital or Polaroid camera (they're making a comeback *squeaks excitedly*!), picture frame for your snappees to smile behind, and props that fit with your fun fun fun theme!

Best for: Mini-budget brides who can't keep their photographers waiting. And pictures with that old-school hand-snapped, slightly-off-kilter quality.

Post-Production

One of the big bugbears of not going with a pro is you don't get the beautiful presentation book at the end. But if yours was kind enough to give you digital copies of your pictures, or whoever captured your day has handed over the goods, there *are* affordable ways to get your own photo books made up.

Hands up: I often write for **LivingSocial** so you could say I'm a bit biased, but one thing I've noticed is that sites like this are rarely short on photo offers. Deals change daily, so it's worth checking back to keep on top of the latest, but there's usually something going whether it's for albums, frames, prints or canvases.

When deals aren't in the offing, try sites like **MyMemory.com**, **Photobox** or **Snapfish**. For something with that extra-special touch though, I really heart the gorgeousness of **MILK Tailor Made Books**. I mean, come on: they wrap them in fabric and seal them with a button. A *button!*

Best for: Blindsidingly beautiful albums that make your jaw – but not the penny – drop.

CHAPTER 14

The Stationery

Paper prettiness that doesn't cost folding money

In *myyy* day, your mum will tell you, no-one used to send save-the-dates – and she's got a point, they are a relatively new invention. But how much damage could a few extra bits of paper do to your budget? Literally hundreds of pounds, as it turns out.

Why? 'Cause it's not uncommon for swish stationery designers to stick you with a £2.50 to £6 *per save-the-date* price tag – even more for some bespoke or especially intricate designs. And let's not forget, bridies, that's *before* you even get to the actual invites. And the orders of service. And the menus, place cards, table plan…

But, 'dah-dah-dah-dah!': nearlyweds, there's no need to go crying into your champers – naturally, there are plenty of things you can do to get your message over to your guests *without* sacrificing style points, or spending over the odds. Hooray!

Before You Start
The main things that bump up your stationery costs aren't going

to blow your mind, but they could seriously inflate your budget. Take note…

The More, The Less Merry

I'm not asking you to leave Nanna Susan on the doorstep just so you don't have to print a place name for her – just bear in mind that what seems like nothing (£3 a card, that's like a coffee!) has to be timesed by the number of people (for place names and orders of service), households (for invites and save-the-dates) or tables (for menus) you're inviting. If your guest list looks anything like ours did, that means £3 per invite can very quickly total £200.

It's Complicated

By complexity of design I'm talking, first of all, letterpress invites. They're trickier to print than flat stationery because they have to go through the press once per colour – so if you can't go flat or digital, at least go monochrome.

Other cost-uppers include things like ribbons, diamantes, hand-stitched envelopes and the latest lust-have look: laser-cut. In case you haven't heard of it, it's that intricately cut-out look used on so many designs – maybe swirls, flowers, words or even people. Check out Hummingbird Cards, Roger La Borde and Rob Ryan if you want to meet the culprits behind my personal laser-cut love.

A New Leaf

Number of pages I mention because some couples like to add handy extra info to invites – maps of the venue location, nearby hotels at various prices, that sort of thing. But there are ways of being Mr & Mrs Helpful (to-be!) without creating complicated concertina invites that set you back £8 apiece. Want to know what they are? Keep reading.

It's So YOU!

As for personalisation, that's up to you. Do it yourself – ideas coming up – and you can have it as so-you as can be without emptying out your drinks fund. Have a bespoke designer create hand-drawn cards in your image or laser-cut your individual silhouettes and you can wave bye-bye to the pre-reception tipple.

It's in the Post
Postage might seem like it can't be helped unless everyone you're inviting is within walking distance, but I've given it some thought and, coming up after the break: a seriously simple way to knock it right down.

Signed, Sealed, Delivered
Not one to shy away from a challenge, I've sorted out some answers to all of the above stationery woes. Now lemme see that smile!

Digi Does It
There's nothing like a paper invite to remind your guests to RSVP – and these days everybody loves receiving *actual* post! But for my money, the same doesn't apply to a save-the-date – and since there's no long tradition of them, I'd say they're okay done online.

As long as you know that most of your friends check Facebook regularly for example, and you can contact ones who don't by text, phone or – shocker! – face-to-face, I'd recommend a quick-smart ping just telling them to get out their diaries, before the proper formal invite comes along in your own time.

Don't want to be forgotten? Take the YouTube route and upload a video of the two of you to a private link.

The Font of All Knowledge
This is my number-one way to shrink down your stationery spend without seeming like Scrooge McMarrieds on the details: your very own, brand-spanking-new wedding website.

Before you start counting up the cost of a dedicated site host etcetera etcetera, note youandyourwedding.co.uk/planning-tools. Full disclosure: I worked in-house at *YYW* for a year so I've got a lot of love for them. But I do know signing up to their planning tools costs you nada, *and* includes your very own wed-site to fill with suggested flights for people coming from afar, taxi numbers for people coming from nearby and all the rest of it to your heart's content. *Without* adding pages to your invites.

The Mail Matriarch
We're right back, after those messages – and here, as promised, is the answer to your postal prayers: she's called the Mail Matriarch, and she's the friend, nan, mum, sister, aunt, or, okay, grandpa, dad, bro or uncle who tends to find themselves at the epicentre of family/friendly life – the one everyone else revolves around, and whose house is the place that everyone pops in and out of at least once a week. Well, that or she's the (slightly nosy, very caring) type who turns up on everyone *else's* doorsteps and invites herself in for inopportune cups of tea.

Because *she will see everyone*. She'll also love the opportunity to have The Knowledge when it comes to your nuptials. And as long as you can trust her not to 'lose' anyone she doesn't like, you can pop everyone's invites into one parcel and just pay the postage to her. Believe me, it *will* be less than First-Classing them all on their own.

Pretty as a Picture
As long as your website is taking care of all the additives, there's no need for your invites to be more than a single page. And that opens up all sorts of options: think about pretty postcards (I'm not talking holiday destinations so much as stylish designs) from some of the brands I'm about to outline. Bought in bulk they can work out cheaper than traditional cards or invites, but still end up super-stylish!

Seasonal Stock
This one works best for winter weddings, but you may find a few off-season specials around Valentine's and post-Easter as well. I'm

thinking Christmas cards – the kind with a happy, loved-up couple and a blank inside – bought in bulk in January and then styled into invites by words in your own fair hand.

The Sum of All Things

As for the rest of it – the menus, place cards and all that – if you can, get it all in one fell swoop, either by the same stationer or as part of your venue package. The drawback with the venue option is you're unlikely to get much say in how it looks, but it's also unlikely to be less than simple and elegant, and it could cut the cost overall. It will vary by venue though, so just double-check how much of your hire fee they're estimating this comes to, and be sure you couldn't get it done yourself for less. When it comes to the stationer, point out that you're putting a lot of work their way, and ask about a discount on the overall price.

The Ultimate in So-You Style

Whether it's you, your fiancé or a friend or family member who has the graphic skills, rope them in to design your dream W-day motif. It could be anything – from flowers to butterflies and hearts to your new family crest – and it can go on *everything* to tie it all together. Then all you need to do is write up the invites, orders of service, menus, table plans, place names etc. and get them printed up at your local print shop. Talk to them about doing you a discount on everything – and whether they'll sell you a job lot of envelopes, too. (Alternatively hit **Wilkos** for your packaging – we got four packs of 25 rustic brown envelopes there for £3.20 total.)

Affordable Brands

If you'd rather not whip up your own designs, by all means, poke your nose in the local stationer's – being a freelancer myself I'm all for supporting independents whenever you can (you miiight have noticed that just a little bit). But if you don't have the good fortune to live around the corner from a calligrapher, here come my favourite affordable names for seriously fabulous stationery. And that *includes* laser-cut styles.

Bride and Groom Direct

Turns out I'm not the only one who thought of the whole postcard-invite thing. Check out Bride and Groom Direct for sweet and simple designs that I've seen start from as little as 48p each. They were good for everything from unfussy illustrations to fun photo invites last time I checked – all available with personalisation, and many for under £1 each. Also check out their invite packs (under Wedding Stationery) for sets of eight invites for as little as £2.19 – that's 37p per person! Expect similarly epic bargains for all the other accoutrements – anyone for eight place cards for 99p?

Carla Jones Design

If a sketchy line drawing is your idea of handmade-minimalist chic, you want the packs of 20 invites at Carla Jones Design. Going for £22.50 when last I looked, they even came with shimmery silver envelopes to add that final glamorous flash.

Clinton Cards

I'm one of *those* people. You know the ones. They linger in your way in card shops for 20 minutes trying to pick *the* perfect one for that person they met that time for all of half an hour. So let's just say I know my way around Clinton's, and I can point you in the direction of their best-bet wedding invites. The ultra-glamorous, beautifully illustrated Deco packs don't seem to be going anywhere fast, and I've spotted them in sets of 10 for £7.50 – they were even available in all-day or evening-only incarnations. Let's do the maths: that's über-elegance for only 75p each.

Confetti.co.uk

Confetti's for-sure a good all-rounder – the place to be for all your stationery, not to mention other bits and bobs like decs and favours. There are some surprising splashes of retro cuteness and understated elegance among the simpler no-frills styles, and you can expect to pay roughly £1.09 (if you're getting more than 249) to £1.69 (for 24 – 44) per standard invitation, and about 58p each for place cards. Oh, and you usually get to choose from four to 10 different colours to boot. Check out the laser-cut section for intricate-yet-affordable accoutrements like glass cards and table numbers.

Cute Maps

Does what it says on the tin! Gorgeous illustrated maps in full colour, half-colour or black and white with a fun, picture-book feel. I'll level with you: invite prices here aren't often on our side, but I've found sets of menus at £32 for 20, place cards at £22 for 40, favour tags at £13.50 for 30 and table name and number cards at £18 for 8 – spot-on for globetrotting types.

Etsy

Sure, there are lots of lovely sellers offering cutesy handcrafted invites at Etsy – would you expect anything less? But the thing I love is that DIY brides without a natural knack for design can buy digital ones to get printed up themselves. Oh, and did I mention I've spied them from a whole 13p apiece?

Folksy

If you're a vintage type, morechic.thanshabby weddings at Folksy will turn your head – their lacy designs with Swarovski detailing and illustrations of old-school silverware have been up for about £1.50 each, and she could do you the rest of your wedding must-haves too if you dropped her a line by email.

More modern nearlyweds *need* to take a moment for Paper and Inc., since their styles are as striking and contemporary-cute as their much more expensive competitors. At the time of writing their bold lovebirds designs were just £1.40 each, while their retro-inspired wordy designs were £1.70. Top tip though: double-check their direct website, paperandinc.co.uk, as you'll find menus and the rest, plus prices can be even cheaper there.

Hallmark

There's sometimes a small selection of wedding-invite postcards that come in under our budget over at Hallmark's UK website – I've spied a double-sided Deco style with hearts and tweety-birds for £1.50 each. Alternatively, if you wanted to keep it seriously simple, there were 10-packs of monochrome invites with simple worded, ribbon headers for £2.99.

Hobbycraft

They're your DIY bride's essential, hands down. You want 50 blank place cards? I've seen 'em for £4.25. Blank menu cards? £2 please. Way to bag everything you need to put together your own handmade styles in one seriously hot spot.

Individual Invites

If 'happy', 'bright' or 'chirpy' are your big-day buzzwords, Individual Invites could be the place to set the tone – last time I was there they were all ditsy florals and cutesie lovebirds with a modern twist. Their double-sided notecard invites were £1.50 each, including envelopes, and a brand new trio of eight-pack save-the-dates and invites were just £8 to £12.

John Lewis

Whether it's totally trad or pure and simple that's your style, John Lewis's wedding selection is about elegance without the fuss. In the past that meant 10 laser-cut butterfly invites for £9, 10 white invites with porcelain-inspired footer motif for £6 and six utterly minimalist, words-only evening wedding invites for £3. They also did a nice line in gold-bordered, plain place cards, 12 for £3, and make-your-own kits with enough gumph for 10 to 15 cards for £5 to £10.

Lily Anna Rose

If trad or regal style's your bag, Lily Anna Rose has all manner of royally classic invites, many of which I've found in packs of 10 for £8 – think delicate borders in gold or silver with slender, looping lettering. They offer orders of service, place cards and the rest too, but most are bespoke and costs vary.

Notonthehighstreet.com

For me, Beautiful Day at Notonthehighstreet is a real find. Many of their adorably illustrated designs have been known to come in under £1.50 per invite – think vintage bikes, birdcages, peacocks and parasols – and some were even less than £1 if you were willing to go with party-style cupcakes and bunting. If there's a girlie, vintage or retro bone in your body, prepare to give your heart away.

Elsewhere, Tigerlily Wedding Stationery and PaperGrace weren't quite as penny-saving on the invite side, but they were great for quirky, pretty, affordable extras like menus and orders of service.

Paperchase

Paperchase, let me count the ways... Remember I mentioned a *slight* obsession with laser-cut (was it really that recently?)? Well, this is where my bargain-loving fellow followers of fabulousness and I get their fix. That's right: I've spotted – and worshipped – 10 printable cards with wraparound laser-cut hearts here that were only £10. As if that wasn't enough, there were also packs of 10 eco-vintage invites with laser-cut-inspired headers for £8. And for from-the-ground-up brides: 10-packs of blank A7 cards with inserts and envelopes were £3, while blank place cards started from £1.75 for 10. *Sigh*

Papernation

This is where that 'postcards' idea comes into its own – especially for you vintage fans. Why give everyone you love identical invitations when you can get the likes of 12 assorted posties on a theme – flora and fauna, butterflies, Paris, New York, London, vintage postcards past – for about £8.95? Oh yeah, and you know that 'seasonal notecards' bit you scoffed at? Boom: mixed boxes of cute, colourful, assorted blank notecards were last seen here for £6.50 to £8.

Paperless Post

Okay, I actually can't get enough of the invites at Paperless Post. And the best news? Some of them are *free*. That's right: nil, nada. Admittedly they're the simpler, not-so-luxe designs, but there's still some prettiness here in the shape of delicate blossom branches and cute line-drawn luggage.

Go up a rung and the seriously sweet designs start to come in – think strings of Japanese lanterns in sherbert shades, looks that mimic telegrams and swirling typography. The last step up is where the big names live – yep, there's stationary by kate spade new york and Oscar de la Renta – but even at this be-still-my-beating-heart stage styles are *still* affordable.

How? The clue's in the name: the Manhattan-based bunch specialise in online invites. They *do* print some paper ones, but I wouldn't want to mess with US postage myself – instead, stick with the virtual beauties and pay by the 'Paperless Post stamp'. Besides the free designs, styles start at 1 stamp each and go up to, er, 2. It's more for premium extras like envelope liners, but you could easily get 100 or more invites out of a pack of 300 stamps. And how much are they, I hear you ask? $26. At the time of writing that amounted to a whole £15.30.

Talking Tables

You may recognise some of Talking Tables' lovely laser-cuts from John Lewis – it's always worth taking a look at both though, just in case there are a few extra items. They do have the simple, elegant invites first described in my JL entry, but as the name suggests, the tableware is where they really shine. Give me the 10 laser-cut bird, heart or butterfly place cards I saw for £4 or £5 any day of the week.

Wedding Soon
Most of Wedding Soon's paraphernalia is of a classic persuasion, and the majority of their invites were out of our price range last time I looked – for floral fans, though, there was a trio of affordable cards featuring roses and peonies for £1.50 each.

What I'd really come here for is the extras – think table numbers featuring lovebirds over a prettily tied ribbon that were £1.80 each; menus to match for £1.40 a pop; or simpler cherry blossom menu cards for a teeny-tiny 50p per print.

Best for: Graphically challenged brides or not-natural-but-determined DIY-ers. Also whirlwind weddings that need something non-bespoke, and need it *now*.

CHAPTER 15

Style Details

Little bits and pieces with teeny-tiny price tags

... Or, the best of the rest. These are my favourite places to find those fiddly little bits and pieces – decorations, guest books, favours, table plans, tableware – that can really add up if you're not on your game. Whatever your style of day – modern, retro or vintage; laidback or super-elegant; off-the wall or understated – these guys can sort you out without you resorting to student suppers (beans on toast, anyone?) in the run-up to married life.

Before You Start
This section's top picks are places nationwide so all you Bs2B can benefit. If you're looking local though, it's haberdashers, homeware stores and gift shops that you want on side – plus the odd charity or antique shop, especially if you're going retro or vintage.

Gift Shops
Lay the table for a quirky, cool or vintage day with vases, favours and cake stands from this little lot.

Out of Love

Stick to the small stuff and they'll see you right at eclectic, vintage-loving online boutique Out of Love. Think five heart-shaped seed papers as favours for £6, or six mini milk bottles as farmyard-style vases for £12.95.

The Handpicked Collection

Modern and chic, quirky and unusual, far-flung and exotic – it's all been specially selected for The Handpicked Collection. A good spot for glassware, candleholders and unexpected extras with that certain *je ne sais quoi*, last time I stopped by I was loving their 'caterpillar bud vase' – a so-now centrepiece that kept your flower costs in check (£9.95).

The Gifted Penguin

Witty or pretty, cool or quirky, you'll find it at The Gifted Penguin. My fave picks at the time of writing: a silvery, vintage-y flower jug as a barn-style centrepiece (£10.99); a cream, three-tier cake stand with lace-look edging (£24.99); and – if you've got a little bit left over – a retro British Puddings print to hang behind your sweetie table (£19.99).

V&A Museum Shop

It goes without saying that the V&A's gift shop is a great stop for old-school touches – in the past I've dug out a vintage pack of 'snap' cards for the kids' table that was £2.50 – but they can also be an unexpected resource for the DIY bride on a heritage kick: think little wooden print blocks for £2.50 each, a roll of flowery fabric tape for £4 and sheets of V&A fabric for £3.50 to £11.50.

Haberdashers

Break out the scissors and glitter-glue – these guys have got everything for a totally handcrafted day, from place cards to cake.

Amazon

Ah Amazon, you strange supermarket on a server – how you stock everything from tissue paper to loveheart stickers and plain white tags to star-shaped hole punches. And how you helped to make my misguided attempt at hand-punching 100 bags of confetti (yes, really) just a helluva lot less painful on my purse (if not my hands). Seriously, check them out before you hit the checkout on one of the more specialised sites – I got 100 tiny wooden pegs (don't ask) for £1.65 when elsewhere I couldn't get them for less than £13.50.

Handmadebyhells

Hells knows you've got favours to wrap, cakes to deck out and places to hold – and that's why she's gone and given us a bridal section all of our very own. Expect tidbits from tuxedo-shaped boxes (last seen at £3.95 for 10) to table gems (were £2.89 for 56g) and faux bundles of baby's breath (about £1.25).

Hobbycraft

The big daddy of make-it-yourself supplies, Hobbycraft has got the lot – coloured card, stationery, food colouring, you name it. In our nuptial neck of the woods I've come across faux-flower corsages for £1.29 each; pearlescent, laser-cut favour boxes, 20 for £6.99; and glass votives for 99p.

Paperchase

Go ahead, make my invite. With art materials straight from Paperchase, that is. They've got everything from paint and paper to washi tape (if you don't know, go and get some now – endless hours of fun!) – even flower-shaped hole punches. On top of all that, in the past I've found pretty painted teapots just begging to be filled with flowers (£8), rose-shaped cake candles for cupcakes and co. (5 for £3) and red-rose floating candles for fishbowl centrepieces (£6 for 9).

Homeware

Whether it's just-for-the-look stuff like ornaments and picture frames or table essentials like plates and glassware, if you can name the room it goes in, you can find it somewhere in here.

Cox & Cox

You'd better be feeling restrained when you click 'Weddings' on the Cox & Cox website – you're about to discover all sorts of things you never knew you needed for your big day, but now can't imagine it without. When I was last there, those things included a 3-metre garland of Moroccan-style lamps (£36), a trio of hyacinth bulb vases (£16.50), cream and purple grosgrain ribbon printed with the words 'to have and to hold from this day forward' (£14.50) and a butterfly hole-punch that even did the little details on the wings (£12.50).

Five Go Mad

If you've got an old-fashioned British afternoon tea on your mind, Five Go Mad is worth a thought. The deliciously bizarre site has been known to collect together curiosities from mini-Union Jack bunting (£10) to nine types of leaf tea presented in little metal canisters (£30) and, for reasons I can't quite fathom, a velvet spaniel toy on vintage Meccano wheels (£38).

HomeArama

Elegance, thy name is HomeArama. I mean, you've gotta love a place that has a whole section just for cake stands. Especially since I've seen them stock a little one for £9.75, a medium one for £14 and a lace-effect one for £17. Worth a peek for display-ware in general, HomeA also had a patterned glass jar for sweeties or cakes for £25 and a pastel pink vase for £9.75.

Lakeland

You know that bit about naming the room? Lakeland's favourite by far is the kitchen. Baker brides come here for the cake decorations and fancy-schmancy serveware – I'd recommend them for the little touches, like the 50 tealights I saw for £2.99, or the 120 doilies in seven designs that were £4.99.

Pale & Interesting
Being as ladida as Pale & Interesting are, many of their wares are a little on the pricey side, but go in small and you can find the occasional affordable gem. At the time of writing, the following fit the bill: a small two-tier pressed-glass cake stand (£8.50), its larger cousin (£10.95) and a triplet of large apothecary jars spot-on for a sweetie table (£39.95). Happy hunting!

Party & Wedding Boutiques
There's nothing like a site that's tailor-made for weddings for having all those finishing touches you forgot that you'd forgotten. From favour bags to glass cards, fill your boots (and your four corners) with the help of all these clever little know-it-alls.

Chloe Beck
Whether you're after a candle with the contours of a wedding cake (£2.29) or a metal bookmark in the shape of a snowflake (£1.59), I've found favours of every flavour over at Chloe Beck. Don't expect said presents for under £1 outside sale time, but there will likely be plenty around the £1.50 to £3 marker. And that's not all they do: you could also pick up affordable cake toppers (most £5.99), packs of 10 or 12 place cards (most £4 to £4.50) and trad-style guest books while you're here too (most £16.97).

Confetti
Few shops know weddings like Confetti, and few can pull off their prices – when you buy in bulk you can get pretty impressive savings on things like place cards and colour-co-ordinated disposable cameras. I've laid eyes on six-packs of mini bonbons in organza bags that were £3.99, 48 – 90 laser-cut rose-shaped

glass cards that were 69p each (79p for fewer, 58p for more) and a build-it-yourself, heavy-card birdcage postbox that was £12.99. Simple as that.

Talking Tables

If it's good enough for John Lewis, it's good enough for me – and they do sell a heck of a lot of Talking Tables goodies. Personal all-time faves have included their floral cake wraps with toppers (£5 for 24 wraps and 15 toppers), laser-cut heart-shaped favour boxes (10 for £7) and laser-cut butterfly place cards (10 for £4.50). Et voilà!

Everything But the Kitchen Sink

Whether they're indie sellers hand-making their crafty cuts out of their kitchens or flower-growers bagging up their petals for confetti, these are my picks of the ultimate places that won't be put in a box.

Bouf

At the time of writing, the first thing that came up on the home-page at Bouf was Paperself Eyelashes. Yup, you read that right: false lashes decked out with everything from butterflies to the London skyline. And that pretty much sets the tone for the rest of the wonderfully loopy boutique – but that's not to say that some of their sellers' goods aren't still super-sweet and romantic. Think the likes of a domed bell jar with pastel base for £15 or a triple-set of white laser-cut vases in three sizes for £8.95. Bananas *and* beautiful.

Dotcomgiftshop

You can search wedding accessories by theme at Dotcomgiftshop. The choices? At last count: white, black and white, pink, and vintage. If your day falls even close to any of those, you're about to be knee-deep in options you can't say no to – but there's actually more here than those cheeky categories let on. For rustic weddings

I've seen four coloured, hanging jam jar tea-light holders for £7.95 and paisley and floral paper bunting for £6.95. For exotic summer afternoons under marquees or in teepees: a 30cm white Moroccan metal lantern for £9.95. For romantic, wintry weddings: four red rose mini-candles in white bowls for £3.95. And the list goes on…

Etsy

Know what you want, or have plenty of time on your hands, and Etsy can be a treasure trove for handmade, rustic or vintage *everything*. Under wedding decorations, categories include the usual cake toppers, decs and favours – but then there are card boxes, signage and photo booth props on top. I've spied 12 paper lips, glasses and 'taches on sticks from Acherryortwo that would have made for fun photos for £6.23; a vintage card-box with lace trim and fabric banner from ThePaperWalrus that was £26.21; and five mini jam jars with fabric and twine covers that were £6 from HuffyHen.

Folksy

Folksy's menagerie of modern British crafters will do you anything from guest books to place cards – even vintage-style button-and-jewellery bouquets. Last time I dropped in, Samantha Geen Designs were personalising guest books with lace, ribbons and buttons for £28, vintage wedding-wishing-tree tags with flowers and birdcages were 35p each from morechic.thanshabby weddings and a quirky-cute bespoke Japanese paper daisy bouquet by Lily Belle Keepsakes was £15.

Notonthehighstreet

Sure, they do everything from tissue-paper pom-poms to hanging heart tea-light holders – they wouldn't be in this section if they didn't – but one of my favourite things about Notonthehighstreet is their cute selection of über-affordable favours. In the past that's included DIY popcorn in plastic cones with personalised stickers and raffia ties, 45p each from bedcrumb; personalised bags of Love Hearts for the same price from Victoria Joy ETC; personalised seaside-style rock lollies by Katie Sue Design Co. for £1.20; and personalised red heart-shaped lollies by Victoria Joy ETC for £1.45 each. *Sweet*.

Papermash

If it's made of paper, pick it up here. At the time of writing, Papermash's pretty pastels freshened up vintage-print doilies (30 in three designs, £4) and gave life to old-school honeycomb wedding bells (£5), while their bookplates in cupcake, owl and typewriter designs made for a beautiful, affordable alternative wedding favour (£4.95 for 12). As if that wasn't enough, vintage-lovers and jetsetters could get on board with 10 old-school travel-themed tags for £4.95.

Pipii.co.uk

Decorate your cupcakes, light up your reception and add colour to your sweetie table in one fell swoop – it's all bunting, butterfly clips, tea-light holders and stripy straws over at Pipii. Last time I looked, your best bets included 18 elegant white favour pouches for £9, a rustic wooden 'wedding' arrow sign for £4.75 and 25 cute red-heart cocktail sticks for £2.75.

Shropshire Petals

What can I say? I didn't want to leave Shropshire Petals out on their own in the wilds of a confetti-only category. So here they are, sneaked into my catch-all cat, even though they specialise solely in real-flower confetti. They just had to have a mention, 'cause the lovely folks behind these flowers not only know their blooms, they've almost always got a special offer going on. The kind of thing you can expect: I've seen two litres (that's 20 handfuls) of any large petal and delphinium mix for £24 (about £1.25 a throw).

Thorntons

They may be no hitherto-unknown indie kids, but then I'm no hipster – and I'd be perfectly happy to turn to some tasty Thorntons for my chocolate favour needs. Check out the Wedding section of their website, where a single chocolate in a lilac and white dotty box has been seen reduced from £1.15 to 58p in the sale. If you've done any kind of favour hunting, you'll know that for a favour *and* the trimmings that really does leave you sitting pretty.

Alternatively, stump up for a chocolate tray – I'd advise going for the wrapped kind then dividing them out. Back when I put keyboard to virtual paper, 1kg of peppermint cremes in silver foil was in the sale for £8 instead of £25 – but even full price it would have worked out well since that made 60 or 70 chocs 38 to 41p each.

Wilkinson

Another name you knew, but never realised was so handy – find glassware, faux flowers and candles for less all at Wilko. They've done 100 tea lights for £2 before, as well as an unscented pillar candle for £2 or the scented version for £2.50, vases from £2.20 and coloured hanging lanterns for £1. Oh, and did I mention that those bell jars you've been after started from just £3.25, and clip-top jam-jars from £1? Just sayin'…

Hire

No room for 20 vases and 100 plates and glasses round at yours 'til the big day? Check out these nationwide hire houses and hand over the hassle to someone else.

Joneshire.co.uk

Jonesey's catering kit covers glassware, china, cutlery, linen – even chairs, tables and coat rails with hangers. Luxe up your marquee or park venue for less than buying with glasses by John Rocha and Jasper Conran, china by Wedgwood and Nina Campbell and chairs so swish you won't need covers. The only thing: I can't price up these guys because they only offer a personalised quote.

Waitrose
If you don't need your glass with panache, pick up the basics on loan from Waitrose for nothing, nada, free. That's right – pop along to the customer service desk and see for yourself: flutes and sherry glasses come in cases of 48, and wine, pint and half-pint glasses in 24s. And the only thing you'll have to pay for is breakages.

Local Lovelies
These are the best nationwide hirers I know. For more options, look up your local events companies – you could get your goods with smaller delivery and collection costs, or pick up in person and cut them out completely.

CHAPTER 16

Inspiration

Now you know the numbers, go forth and get your ideas on

Go now, be free! *Sniff, sniff* Don't come back! I hate you, I hate you! Be free, be free! Because I like to think my little book has taught you soon-to-be-weddeds everything you need to know to keep your pennies in your purse and still get some style on your aisle. But if you could use a little more inspiration, be it in the theme, scheme, or anything-else-visual departments, I can point you in the direction of some clever clogs who'll be happy to help you continue your *sniff* journey without me.

Wedding Magazines
There are a million and one of these things out there, and when I first got engaged, I bought them all. Of course, that was before I went to work at *You & Your Wedding*, then later started writing freelance for *Brides*, and learned to spot real joy-to-read quality.

Lucky really, since I love both mags – they're fab for ideas and advice on everything from what to do with your fancified coiff to bridal gown styles that are so now, and from pretty, alternative centrepieces to quirky ways to lay your table. I know my thousands of words will have got your creative brains a-whirrin', but sometimes you've just got to see it to believe it.

If it's local knowledge you're down on though, I'd add your nearest edition of *County Wedding Magazines* to the pile you take to the till at WHSmith. They're a great resource for venues and suppliers right on your doorstep – and they'll save you tonnes of time in Google searches.

The Belles of the Blogs

Lest we forget, I had nigh-on four years to ponder my big day – and I had to fill the quiet, saving-not-spending evenings with something to satisfy my obsession. Cue my five favourite wedding blogs…

OMG I'm Getting Married may be one of the prettiest wedding blogs in Britain. I mean, come on, you can tell it's put together by a graphic designer. If you want to while away your nights rifling through sumptuous real weddings and engagement shoots, just soaking up the eye candy, this is the blog for you.

Rock My Wedding is another über-good-looking blog – think giant photos of weddings and stationery, cakes and favours and some totally doable DIY. The clan behind RMW are cool, in a totally approachable way – and their writing style is relaxed and friendly, just like talking to an excited, wedding-savvy mate.

Annabel at **Love My Dress** has her finger on the pulse of bridal fashion – whether it's Minna and Phase Eight (great minds!) or the inspiring stylings of Claire Pettibone and State of Grace. Her blog's also worth a look for hair and beauty tips and ideas – perfect if you're drafting in a BM for your W-day…

Georgia at **Before the Big Day** divvies up her real weddings by theme – and among the usual 'urban', 'vintage' and 'marquee' are smile-on-your-face surprises. After something quirky? She'll show you how other brides used antlers, black veils, fans and light-up dance-floors in their wedding days. Worried about the weather? Check out the smiles on her rainy-day brides' and grooms' faces.